INDEPENDENT STUDY

Bold New Venture

INDEPENDENT STUDY

STUDY

Bold New Venture

Edited by

DAVID W. BEGGS, III

and

EDWARD G. BUFFIE

INDIANA UNIVERSITY PRESS

BLOOMINGTON & LONDON

SECOND PRINTING 1966

Preface

Bold New Venture Series

AMERICAN education is emerging as a new frontier. Staggering challenges brought about by the contemporary demand for quality education for a bulging and diverse student population must be met. Old solutions for new problems will not suffice.

Pioneer educators are testing promising new programs and practices to effect fundamental improvement in the schools. Healthy dissatisfactions have led to the belief that if the schools are to be significantly better, they will have to be substantially different. Both the substance and the form of instruction are undergoing searching reappraisal. Exciting innovations have been instituted in schools scattered throughout the country. The *Bold New Venture* series is designed to inform educators and the interested public about these new developments and to assist in their evaluation.

The books in this series differ from much of the professional literature in education. The contributors, for the most part, are practitioners. Admittedly they are partial to their topics. Nevertheless, pitfalls are exposed and candid treatment is given to the issues. Emphasis has been put on reporting *how* as well as *why* new practices and programs were inaugurated. The volumes in this series are intended to be a stimulus to the conversation which must take place if fresh methods of teaching are to find their way into the schools.

Topics included in the *Bold New Venture* series include team teaching, flexible scheduling, independent study, the nongraded school, instructional materials centers, data processing, small group instruction, and technological aids.

While journalists criticize, scholars theorize about, and philosophers analyze education, the teachers of America must act. Educators must leap from theory to practice in individualizing instruction. More responsibility must be given and accepted by youngsters for their own learning. Intellectual inquiry must become full-time, leisure-time, and life-time pursuits.

Progress in education does not always come by the process of addition with more teachers, more books, more courses, and more money. Real improvement can come from original uses of scarce human talent, precious time, and new methods.

Because it is intended primarily for teachers and administrators, the *Bold New Venture* series focuses on the practical problems of teaching. What has been operationally successful for some teachers may have application for other teachers. If new practices or programs result from these books, then the series will have fulfilled its aim, for the *Bold New Venture* books are calls and guides to action.

Bloomington, Indiana   D.W.B.

                                                                    E.G.B.

Contents

Introduction

THIS BOOK is concerned with independent study, long a stepchild of the instructional process used in most American schools. Tradition, expediency, and folklore have led to organizing the schools around one teacher for every twenty-five or so youngsters. With this organization the teacher does most of the talking, and hopefully the students are nearly always listening. In such a situation the student is led to be highly dependent on the teacher. When the student is stirred into action, it usually is in response to a teacher objective and directive. Seldom have most students given much more than has been requested of them in academic affairs.

Most frequently what the teacher talks about comes from the textbook. Written for students differing in reading skills and comprehension abilities, basic textbooks have a pronounced tendency to oversimplify and generalize. After all, the publishers reason, books must be produced to suit a range of attitudes, pet interests, and cherished beliefs about the content of every course. A little something for everyone has too long been the formula for textbook construction.

The school's class schedule, its operational manifestation of how youngsters learn, is frozen into an equal distribution of time, class size, and assignment of teachers and pupils. There is a preoccupation with unreasoned equality. All students get the same amount of time and instruction in one subject as in all others. This equates the teaching-learning process in a complex, difficult subject with an easy, simple one. A different design for learning is required for increased quality in education.

Sweeping Reforms

American public education must make sweeping changes. The schools must provide learning opportunities which satisfy the unique

ix

requirements of each individual. Independent study should be the learning procedure used by every student in every school. The able and ambitious learner must be freed from the oversimplified text. At the same time, the youngster without scholastic ability must be unshackled from unreasonable academic demands.

It is a less difficult undertaking to identify problems and call for reform than it is to institute programs to nullify even the accepted criticisms. However, this book presents alternate plans for increasing the use of independent study in elementary and secondary schools. Independent study, broadly conceived, is a way of learning in which the student focuses attention on a specific organizing idea or a body of knowledge and masters it at his own rate of understanding. The wholesale use of independent study is a means through which teachers can satisfy the individual learning needs of students. It places emphasis on self-regulation and self-responsibility for learning.

Quality Education

To achieve added quality in American public schools, school programs must pay increased attention to the differences between students. Quality education results from quality instruction. What is needed is not, as some have suggested, more and tougher courses. The number of youths who leave school early, the low achievement scores on standardized tests of a large number of youngsters, and the reports of dissatisfaction and frustration from students are evidence that added rigor is not the road to quality education. At the same time, it is obvious to firsthand observers in the schools that some students should do more and different academic work. Independent study is a practical way to increase the worth of American education for all youth.

Changing Knowledge

Knowledge is not a stable thing. It is like a live emerging organism. If this is doubted, visit an elementary school classroom during instruction in modern mathematics. Listen to the contemporary problems in a junior high social studies class. Read the latest information dealing with high school chemistry. There are other telling examples. For instance, the typical physical theory goes out of date in about ten years. In many industries ninety percent of the products produced today were unknown a decade or so ago. Likewise, the technology which produces them is equally new. The future promises to yield as many if not more changes in knowledge. These developments are the result of fresh thinking, thinking independent from the beliefs of the past. The schools must be educating for change. Because all of the schools' resources, human and material, need to be aimed at developing each youngster to the limits of his capability, instruction should focus on the individual.

Psychology and a Lesson

Educational psychology, a relatively new field, has just begun to unlock the secret of how people learn. Psychologists have painted a clear picture of the kinds of learning that are possible and the variations of potential among human learners. School programs should be organized to reckon with these human differences.

Some educational psychologists have stressed the importance of activity in learning. People learn by doing. Using processes and handling knowledge are the means to acquisition. Stress is laid on the need for success in academic pursuits if the student is to perpetuate a desire to learn. Independent study, properly carried out, can be a means whereby youngsters use a full range of processes and knowledge in a manner that is personally successful and satisfying.

Independent Study: A Powerful Concept

The word *independent* has dynamic connotations. It implies self-determination and personal identification. To be independent, one must be responsible and self-sufficient. Each of these qualities should be a part of any defensible list of educational objectives. *Study* implies enlightenment and, hopefully, development. No man can do this for another. No teacher can do this for a student.

The whole notion of *independent study* has therefore powerful implications for the person engaged in it. Too much teaching in the past has been concerned with description and rote learning; too little attention has been given to analysis and reflection. The single teacher, with course syllabus in the drawer and textbook in hand, and the thirty students sitting row upon row before her have been barred from the opportunities and pleasures of independent study in many schools.

The limited experience students have had with independent study has largely been relegated to after hours' homework, when neither the resources of the school nor the assistance of the teacher is at hand to aid the after hours' learner. Independent study, if it is to realize its promise, must be a part of, not apart from, the regular school activity. Several of the following chapters will present exciting models of how this has been done in schools.

Emphasis in this book is placed on ways of developing favorable faculty attitudes and presenting ways teachers can inaugurate independent study activities. If changes are to be brought about in a school, the place to begin is with the teachers. It is the teacher who makes the difference in every school. Little will happen unless the teacher wants something different and better to occur.

Teams, Flexibility, Nongradedness, and Independent Study

Though educators have talked a good deal about the value and need for individualizing instruction, few practical means have been implemented to accomplish this goal. While group instruction is logically valid for some instructional functions, there is a demand in every good school program for youngsters to work on their own in developing skills, systematizing knowledge, and thinking critically.

Recently, several bold new proposals have been made for organizing the school differently. One such proposal calls for the use of teaching teams. A team of more than one teacher becomes responsible for the selection of content and learning experiences and makes the instructional prescription and evaluation of a given group of students. Another proposal, the Trump Plan,[1] advocates the use of a flexible schedule of time, in addition to other procedures. The nongraded school concept, whereby a student moves through the study of content at his own rate unrestrained by grade-level placement, has been widely considered. Each of these reform programs places learning emphasis on independent study. As a school faculty considers one of these school organizations, careful attention to independent study is required.

This Book

Research on independent study in the elementary and secondary schools is limited, as will be noted in the first chapter. The void in the research should ring a bell for the researchers, but it should not dissuade practitioners from inaugurating independent study programs. Reasons for this contention are forcefully given in Chapter One and elsewhere. A similar void exists in the research which puts a positive value on traditional teaching methodology.

Descriptions of successful independent study practices, as viewed by teachers and observers, are reported throughout this book. The positive judgments of educators who have dealt with independent study programs as teachers, administrators, and observers are the best cornerstones available for further implementation of independent study. The best test of an innovation is the test of time. Independent study practices which have stood the test of time are described.

This book, then, deals with:

1. the nature of independent study.
2. the goals of self-assumed learning activities.
3. the ways schools can organize to get independent study into the mainstream of the school program.

Each chapter is a challenge, a charge to educators to consider and to implement some kind of independent study program. The suggestions made are not theoretical models filled with practical difficulties. Instead, the plans presented are realistic guides to action.

This book should be a stimulus for thought for in-service and pre-service educators as they work to make the schools even better. Liberal references, particularly in chapters three through six, are made to specific school programs that are already in operation. Hopefully their presentation will be a source of inspiration to others. Each model presented has a variety of elements which can be redistributed to formulate other models for application in different school settings.

If the schools are to continue to improve their quality, it will probably be through the extension of more opportunities for independent or self-directed study. All of the materials, facilities, and even teachers are of little value if a youngster does not have the opportunity and the challenge to use them, to form ideas from them, and to develop his own skills and understandings.

Concrete examples of school organizations to accommodate independent study are presented in Chapter Seven. For the skeptic who maintains that the traditional way of organizing a school is an eternal law, other specific school organizations are presented.

The eighth chapter is a report from one teacher who has had experience in working with depth independent study. Those who believe in the integrated knowledge approach to learning will be pleased with this chapter.

In Chapter Nine attention is given to the use of multimedia teaching aids for independent study. The reader may learn that the facility requirements are not as great as expected in Chapter Ten. New uses of existing technology and space are suggested.

Chapter Ten deals with the in-service program to transform a traditional program into one which emphasizes independent study. Suggestions for such a program are made.

The Future

Teachers are more than taskmasters when independent study is adopted in a school. Teachers will become friendly companions for learning, consultants on problems, and sources of data for student use. Independent study will require a searching reappraisal of the relationship, as the authors point out, between student and teacher. To the teacher the student's individual accomplishments and intellectual development will be a source of professional pleasure and personal satisfaction. The teacher's role will be expanded far beyond the traditional expectations in group teaching situations.

Also, facilities will change as independent study increases in the school. Space will be provided for individual work, free of the confusion of group activity and the interruptions of others. Furthermore, the single text will be replaced by scores of other materials for study; films, learning programs, recordings, and other data sources gradually will replace the basic text as the reference source.

Independent study is a theme with infinite variations. And all are aimed at making the school experiences of every learner more profitable and enduring. There is much to be done to make the goal of quality education a reality for each individual student. But this is a period of change, of progress in American education. The call to increase the use of independent study is clear and undeniable in its potential advantage for all the children of all the people.

ACKNOWLEDGMENTS

Cooperative ventures place important demands on each of the participants. The editors must express appreciation to the contributors who made this cooperative venture so very worthwhile. The planning, arranging, discussing, reviewing and, sometimes, redoing for this was done with care and dispatch by each of the contributors.

The imperfections contained herein are the responsibility of the editors. What has been done has been guided by their decisions, right or wrong.

Special acknowledgment must be given to the editors' wives, JoAnn Beggs and Patricia Buffie. They helped directly and indirectly. In addition to valuable consultation, they handled many of the laborious details involved.

Gratitude must be expressed to Dr. J. Lloyd Trump, Associate Secretary, National Association of Secondary School Principals, who provided the inspiration to make this project a reality.

Helpful criticism was given by Mr. and Mrs. Peter Casagrande. The final typing chores were handled with dispatch by Mrs. Judy Tish. Miss Jane Rodman of the Indiana University Press gave both her talent and energy to sharpen this manuscript.

Finally, to our teachers, colleagues, and students a word of gratitude is expressed for their assistance, ideas, and examples. Each were a part of the sum that is reflected in what we say and do.

Bloomington, Indiana   D.W.B.
                                                        E.G.B.

INDEPENDENT STUDY

Bold New Venture

CHAPTER 1

Schedules, Bells, Groups, and Independent Study

by

WILLIAM M. GRIFFIN

A pioneer in planned independent study programs, William M. Griffin has been associated with the Wayland School Department in Massachusetts during the development of its nationally recognized program. His doctor's dissertation at Syracuse University was on the subject of independent study. In addition to Syracuse University, he has attended Marietta College in Ohio and the College of Education, State University, Albany, New York. Currently Dr. Griffin is on the faculty of Boston College.

To PRODUCE students who are effective in independent study is what education should be all about. Independent study is not just a feature of organizational or curriculum change which can be added to or deleted from the school's program.[1] It is the system of self-instruction in which each individual learner operates within the total system of the school's instruction. That these two systems are interdependent comes as no news to the astute practitioner bent on developing an independent study program. That there is need to explore the dimensions of these systems for factors which really make a difference also comes as no surprise.

What does it mean to be effective in independent study? How do you know? What are the conditions? How do they relate? One way of exploring the process of independent study is to set forth what

1

effective students do in this kind of learning situation. It is possible to find many statements in the literature related to independent study which cite operational practices associated with the idea of independent study. These practices when edited for duplication of thought, overlapping of meaning, clarity of expression, and grouped into natural clusters, suggest a systems approach to the job of defining the process of independent study.

Approximately one hundred and fifty practices were collected, edited, and grouped into natural sub-trait clusters by the author. It was found that seven clusters would contain all of the practices. The definition contains five examples of practices to exemplify each sub-trait. These are the five ranked highest in importance by jury validation.

Independent Study

The term independent study means a learning situation within the school day which allows a student to develop personal competencies through experiences as an individual but in interaction with others when needed. It is characterized by freedom from constant supervision. Students read, write, contemplate, listen to records and tapes, view, record, memorize, create, build, practice, exercise, experiment, examine, analyze, investigate, question, discover, and converse. Independent study emphasizes the individual's role in learning. It implies that all students possess potentialities for self-initiative, self-discipline, resourcefulness, productivity, and self-evaluation. In this respect, a student performing effectively in independent study is one who:

PERCEIVES WORTHWHILE THINGS TO DO: *for example,* pursues instructional leads for further study, compares various sources of information, asks relationship-type questions, integrates information from different subject-matter fields, summarizes findings and places them in correct frame of reference.

PERSONALIZES LEARNING: *for example,* casts about for a project of real interest and value, gives own unique reasons for doing what is done, prepares a plan to structure the study, distributes work schedule to allow for other commitments, expresses satisfaction in a task of own selection and implementation.

EXERCISES SELF-DISCIPLINE: *for example,* accepts limits of the school without denying self, displays sustained and conscientious industry, seeks procedural authority for own point of view and actions, works in harmony with others in groups of two or three, cooperates in maintaining a climate for individual work.

MAKES USE OF HUMAN RESOURCES: *for example,* initiates contacts with teachers, shares interpretations, interests, and ideas with a teacher in good exchange, comes prepared for conference discussions, uses contacts with teachers to clarify thinking with pertinent and relevant questioning, investigates suggestions which are offered.

MAKES USE OF MATERIAL RESOURCES: *for example,* broadens own knowledge through related readings, makes use of tapes, records, and projectuals to expand knowledge, displays deftness in locating library materials, recognizes and uses the tools of the trade, constructs special materials and devices for use in one's work.

PRODUCES RESULTS: *for example,* works at appropriate pace and follows through to completion, plans projects which are subject to accomplishment, states clear objectives, displays habit of getting down to work, finds application for a creative idea.

STRIVES FOR IMPROVEMENT: *for example,* seeks advice from competent people, corrects errors on own, studies authoritative sources for best practices, uses group sessions to test out ideas and clarify issues, evaluates material in light of personal experiences and firsthand knowledge.

These experiences under independent study may be either related or unrelated to course requirements.

The parts of this chapter that follow deal essentially with the conditions in the school's environment believed to foster independent study. Discussion will be directed to the relationship of independent study to the school's system of instruction (schedules, bells, and groups), and to various other components of the school's instructional system.

The Student's Schedule and Independent Study

A student needs to have control of a substantial amount of his own time in school, and he should have this available to him in time modules appropriate for a variety of tasks. It takes time to read a book, to retrieve information from the library, to define a problem, to hold conferences, to exchange ideas, and to refine one's work.

Traditionally, the schedule maker has tried to avoid assigning a student to a study hall for more than a single period at a time. Now it is apparent that for many independent study purposes longer periods of time are not only desirable but also sometimes necessary. When the independent study portions of a student's week are developed in blocks of time and scheduled in spaces not used for classroom instruction, there is no necessity for the student in independent study to be interrupted by the classroom bell schedule. Examples of schedules which facilitate the use of independent study as the method of learning are given in Chapter Seven.

This ringing of bells has been the time-honored way to signal the beginning and end of classroom periods. Usually this has affected the entire student population in very much the same way. The rigidity with which students have been locked into this type of organization has, of course, become objectionable. The question as far as independent study is concerned is not whether bells ring or no bells ring. It is what the bell means to each individual in the school that counts. If it means something different from one individual to another, it would seem we are headed in the right direction.

For the most part, the things students do during their independent study time represent experiences which cannot be scheduled by the administration. Many students prefer to learn creatively—by questioning, experimenting, risking, testing, and modifying ideas. Educators must have faith enough in these young people to permit and encourage this to happen. Independent study opens improved ways of individualizing instruction.

The Teacher's Schedule and Independent Study

A teacher needs to have control of a substantial amount of his own time in school in order to have the necessary flexibility to arrange individual conferences with students and to engage in professional preparation and planning. This is the interaction level between teacher and pupil and between teacher and teacher which lies beyond the mechanics of the master schedule. Here success depends to a large extent upon fresh diagnostic data. The teacher must see his role as that of motivating, encouraging, and helping the student to make effective use of the many resources around him. Independent study has been called education by appointment. The use of human resources in the process of independent study cannot be "scheduled" by the school in the usual sense of the word. Human resources can only be mobilized by those directly involved.

Independent study is not study carried out by a student entirely on his own. When a student is seeking procedural authority, defining a problem, developing ideas, testing points of view, taking certain risks, he needs to feel the undergirding influence of a teacher whom he respects. A skillful teacher can provide the right amount of help at a time when it is needed most and thus prevent a student engaging needlessly in large amounts of unproductive activity. In this role, the teacher counsels, advises, and plans. This is discussed in some detail in Chapters Five and Eight.

The availability of a teacher to a student engaged in independent study is increased when teachers work in teams. Under a team arrangement within a block of time or on a distributed schedule throughout the day, there is a great possibility that a student may find one of his teachers available. From a scheduling point of view, this is important. If independent study is to flourish in our schools, students should be given every opportunity possible to brush with exciting teachers. This is where the incentive for independent study rubs off.

Group Instruction and Independent Study

Independent study probably thrives best when group instruction is of an "open system."[2] When conducted for a period of several weeks an instructional unit can provide a host of leads for individual pursuit. If a teacher is to perceive his classroom group as individuals, in planning the study of a topic, an issue, a problem, or a theme he should first raise the question: What in this unit can students learn best by themselves? To resolve this question calls for acquaintance with individual students, cooperative planning, and some ideas for individual projects. The author has found that materials written for teacher use are sometimes helpful to students as they are casting about for a project of real interest and value.[3] The concept that students are at times their own teachers is sometimes taken lightly.[4] However, independent study is built on this premise.

Students vary in their ability to perceive worthwhile things to do. Guilford calls this trait "sensitivity to problems" and has developed scales for its measurement.[5] Teachers who are sensitive to this kind of individual difference in students will make a special effort to help certain students get started.

Large group instruction with its multimedia impact serves to create ideas for independent study. In the area of the arts it is particularly effective to alert students to possibilities for developing their individual interests and talents. Independent study in the arts has particular significance for those students unable to elect courses in this area.

Independent study may be related to group instruction in other ways. This relationship can take one of several forms. Students in an "honors program" are sometimes excused from classes, but they continue to work with their teachers who act as consultants. In other instances, a formal tutorial arrangement between teacher and pupil is worked out; here the dialogue can strengthen the independent work. There are examples of contract plans and released time in which occasional checks with the group are a stimulant. Giving individual assignments to students within classes is an obvious approach to encouraging independent work. Another plan whereby pupils actually spend time each Saturday on a college campus in seminar work has been successful. This kind of experience gives incentive to pupils in small high schools. In any of these arrangements reports from schools indicate that students need access to a teacher or group activity in order to keep going.

Spaces and Facilities and Independent Study

Secondary schools have been so completely scheduled with group instruction over the past half century that they have neglected to consider the potential of individual students to schedule themselves. They are expected to do this when they go to college, yet they have had little experience to sustain them.

If students are to take responsibility for their own learning throughout the school day, they must have access to appropriate spaces and facilities. In general, they should find the spaces and facilities for independent study to be open, staffed, and ready for use during all hours of the school day. Independent study facilities occupy a position in school life similar to that of service centers in community life. When we go to a store during business hours, we expect to find it open. When a student has need to use the language lab, for example, he should expect to find it open. Other facilities which fall into the same category of "open" utilization include: resource centers, libraries, programmed materials, study carrels, laboratory bench space, practice rooms, exercise rooms, testing services, audiovisual devices, conference spaces, guidance services, and specialized workshops and studios. Schools providing these facilities in their instructional environment should go further and make sure that they are available to students throughout the whole day.

The Development of Competency and Independent Study

Webster defines the word "independent" as: "having or forming a competency, . . . hence, self-reliant, self-confident, self-respecting, . . . not subservient." These meanings are descriptive of the learner. In independent study it is not the study that is independent, it is the learner that is independent. Reasoning in this manner, an individual engaged in independent study is a person becoming competent in a particular choice of endeavor. Do we think of a high school pupil in the sense of becoming competent? Does he think of himself this way?

In life, outside of school, when we meet a person who is an outstanding performer, we tend to take for granted certain things about him and how he got that way. We express ourselves like this: "I wonder who helped him get his start? He must have studied with a fine teacher. Think of the hours he must have practiced." Are not these dimensions of independent study? Competence as motivation is an intriguing theory to support the conduct so often observed in a person engaged in independent study.

Evaluation and Independent Study

Independent study is a natural way to learn. It need not be restricted by subject-matter boundaries. There is nothing superficial about it. The learner owns what he does and what he has learned how to do. His experiences are as ungraded as life itself. The very nature of the work is a function of a personalized plan which calls for personalized evaluation and reporting.

The effective student in independent study is one who produces results and strives for improvement. The school should report both of these aspects to parents, college admissions officers, employers, and to interested members of the general public. Too, the student should be in a position to show what he has accomplished in his independent study endeavor. The art student who goes to be interviewed with portfolio in hand suggests a cue as to how to do this. Why should not a poem, a research paper, a painting, a project, a model, a write-up of an original experiment, a musical composition, a short story, a publication, a physically fit body, a piece of sculpture, a specimen of typing, a special device, or some other evidence of the quantity and quality of independent study be used as evidence of a productive high school experience? Placing a high value on student effectiveness in independent study and rewarding it when it occurs, the school will have little difficulty in establishing independent study as an integral part of each student's individual schedule. Teachers too will redefine their jobs to include the role of consultant to individual students and to accept the idea that young people are capable of vast amounts of learning apart from them. Parents and community people will also be encouraged to place as much value on a student's independent study time as they place on regular classroom instruction.

CHAPTER 2

Independent Study is Self-Directed Learning

by

WILLIAM M. ROGGE

William M. Rogge has spent the last three years visiting Illinois schools and working with public school educators in the State of Illinois Special Study Project for Gifted Children. He received his doctorate in education from Southern Illinois University and is a professor in the College of Education at the University of Illinois.

THE PERTINENT questions to ask about independent study deal with who chooses what to be learned, what activities students actually carry on, what expectations faculty and students have of themselves and of each other, what products are produced, who does the evaluation, what is evaluated, who participates, what resources are required, what is the relationship to the total school program, and what research supports the various models.

Presently most of the answers must come from programs in colleges and universities. Most of the existing literature describes and evaluates the models in higher education. Articles about independent study in elementary and secondary schools are just beginning to ripple through publications used by the practitioner, under such sections as learning centers, library services, and projects. Little is to be found in research journals.

Several collating and summary efforts have been made. In a United States Office of Education pamphlet Baskin used the following definition as his guideline in choosing activities for examination:

Independent study is defined . . . as independent work or reading, sometimes on one's own, sometimes in small groups [*sic*], but with such work taking place in the absence of the teacher and in lieu of certain regularly scheduled class meetings.[1]

Researchers at the College of Wooster used this definition in selecting twenty programs for study:

An independent study program is one which provides a formal opportunity on an institution-wide basis for the pursuit of special topics or projects by individual students, under the guidance of faculty advisors, apart from organized courses, for honors only or for credit toward graduation, available to students who meet certain requirements or required of all students.[2]

The second definition, while similar to the first, stresses that the independent study activities must be sustained and well enough integrated to be called a program.

One of the early experimenters with independent study, E. E. Robinson,[3] gives an account covering the first six years of the independent study program at Stanford University. The program began in 1925 and initially consisted of a few junior and senior students, high in academic achievement, doing special work guided by faculty advisors. A final examination was given, along with credit toward a degree. Thirteen students graduated under the plan from 1925 through 1928. Then the program was greatly expanded in 1931. The actual work done by the student consisted of reading, writing, and some oral expression. There was not agreement on whether the content was to be supplementary to course work or independent of it. As the program developed, some important changes were made. Individual student-advisor conferences gradually gave way to small group-advisor conferences. The program moved down to the freshman level. Some of the departments, starting initially to give considerable freedom, drew the students back into more typical coursework requirements.

In the view of twenty-two of the Stanford instructors, the program's advantages were an earlier awakening of intellectual interest, acceleration, nurture of the ability to integrate knowledge, and an awakening of scholastic interests. The problems seen were procrastination, inadequate faculty guidance, and overspecialization.

Robinson thought that the Stanford Plan grew out of a concern to arouse more intellectual interest among the superior students. In practice Robinson suggests: "The primary aim of all independent study has been to stimulate the superior student to do more work and better work than he would ordinarily do without individual supervision."[4]

The account of Hatch and Bennett[5] covers much of the postwar expansion in honors and independent work. While many colleges and universities had elements of independent study in their course work, the idea of student repsonsibility for what he wanted to learn constantly darted in and out among the many administrative arrangements called honors and independent work.

It seems fair to say that elementary and secondary schools are in the back swell of a large and important change in college undergraduate instruction from which the schools can profit. Colleges discovered that independent study, first limited to superior seniors, was even more appropriate, in the judgment of most reviewers, for lower classmen of varying academic abilities.

Currently elementary and secondary schools are discovering that greater self-directedness is at least a working hypothesis for their students. The idea of student responsibility for learning is being shaped into working educational programs. The idea fits into the general view that students are capable of more productive thinking if their energies are directed less toward regurgitating what textbooks and teachers tell them and more toward integrating their own experiences and points of view of the world within limits of materials and expectations set by the teacher. Reflecting the general point of view that supports independent study, Barzun states, "Instructors are required to do too much lecturing and students too much sitting and note-taking; both groups should do more independent work and come together for periods of free tuition and apprenticeship."[6]

In beginning the use of independent study on the college level, high achieving students start the program and then typically it is opened to other ability levels. Later made into a required program, some students have a choice about enrolling. Students are generally considered able or unable to do the work, and thus little attention is given to nurturing students into a readiness for independent work. In voluntary programs the general view is that a student is ready at a particular grade level; and when a program is extended, it typically is done a grade level at a time. This latter practice is paradoxically contrary to the elaborate selection practices some schools will use upon their students at a particular grade level.

The two general practices in Illinois high schools, with which the author is most familiar, are either to select students by the same criteria that are used for academically talented classes or to require it of all students at a particular grade level. Neither method has much to commend it. As will be noted later in some of the research, academic aptitude is a low predictor for success in independent study. And to assume that all students are ready for independent study at a particular grade level reveals a conspicuous nonchalance to differences among students.

The imposition of independent study upon all students typically accompanies the various team teaching approaches. However, the students expect to use this time to do their homework growing out of classroom assignments. The students' responsibility is nothing more than doing the drills, reading, and exercises expected of him by adult authority. He is not asked to set some goals for himself but to accept those handed to him by others.

The summary by the Wooster group[7] of twenty selected programs in higher education showed that the voluntary programs have several bases for selection. The most common combination of criteria is a B grade point average or better, approval by the department involved, and certification by a committee in charge of the program.

One of the important unknowns about both college and public school programs is the individual adjustments that teachers, advisors, and faculty members make for individual students. Some of the implied criticism voiced above about admission by class level would need to be softened if reliable evidence could demonstrate that the guidance and supervision offered to the students was truly adjusted to the capacity and needs of the student. Undoubtedly some instructors do this very well, but until the in-service education of the faculty and teachers supports an examination of who expects what of which students, these adjustments will be left haphazardly to the accidents of selection of advisors and students and of assignments of students to advisors.

The Elements of Independent Study

One of the clearest pictures of the nature of independent study is reproduced below from the Wooster report.[8]

TYPES OF INDEPENDENT STUDY PROJECTS DONE
BY STUDENTS IN TWENTY INSTITUTIONS

Type of Project	Type Reported by Senior Students	Type Reported by Faculty Advisors
Information gathering and analysis based on library work only	145	121
Information gathering and analysis involving laboratory or field work	58	30
Artistic creation and/or performance	12	26
Administrative work, counseling, or teaching	0	5
Self-study	12	12
Designing and/or building project	0	1
No information	2	1
Regular course work	0	4
Unclassified	0	29
Total	229	229

The perceptions of faculty advisors and students are fairly close as seen in the report. The twenty-nine unclassified responses of the faculty were so designated because they had no predominate kind of activity to supervise. The library work ranged from summaries of textbook materials to original work with primary sources.

The advisors reported in their interviews that the type of supervision they gave consisted of individual conferences about one third of the time, interim written work one fourth of the time, group meetings or seminars one fourth of the time, directing the student to reading from prescribed lists and a few other activities. The conferences varied from as often as one a week for one fourth of the students to a few students and faculty who seldom or never had conferences. The time for them ranged from a few minutes to an hour.

Most of the twenty undergraduate colleges studied in the above report gave credits ranging from zero to three semester hours to sixteen hours. In addition, the students enjoyed many privileges not available to other students, such as arrangements of course work, admission to graduate seminars, exemption from some examinations, unlimited class cuts, access to library stacks, admission to special libraries, use of carrels and laboratory facilities, and of course strong recommendations by the faculty.

In the Illinois Special Study Project for Gifted Children of 1959, studies and surveys were made of all the elementary and secondary school programs in the state for academically talented children. Only rarely was an honors program described that was not simply a college level course brought into the high school. The number of students reached was extremely small. The few honors courses that did encourage independent work typically were associated with one or two academic areas and were for seniors only.

The independent study associated with team teaching was just getting underway. The writer's experience in two workshops devoted to introducing team teaching indicated that the teachers' prime concern was to handle the lectures well. Small-group discussions or seminars were shrugged off as being easy to handle, because, after all, did they not simply represent a smaller class? Teachers saw them as a situation they had always looked forward to and about which there need be no apprehension. Independent study was almost entirely relegated to homework done, to be sure, in somewhat different physical settings. Only as these team teaching approaches have matured, such as those modeled after the Trump Plan,[9] has more serious attention been given to a new conception of independent study.

Not only team teaching but also learning centers, as described in the January, 1964, issue of *Educational Leadership,* are getting more attention. In the learning centers the traditional library resources and the newer media of communication, such as tapes for tape recorders, film strips, reading laboratories, and special enrichment units are located. The staff serves both in the old role of helping students meet the demands of their classroom assignments and in the new roles of doing remedial work, counseling, and supervising and guiding independent study through case conferences.

In independent study no clearly established and generally accepted policies exist for grading and evaluation, nor can it be reported just what the bases for evaluation consist of. Research into the criteria that faculty and teachers actually use in evaluation would give considerable help in understanding the nature of independent study. The reports show a wide range of practices in grading. Sometimes narrow, specialized examinations are given; sometimes broad comprehensive examinations are used. One of the most unusual approaches is that of Antioch[10] where the student himself is the topic. He evaluates his college experiences, his future role, and the contributions of the college. No grade is given, the work is required, and credit is given. Some programs simply give a pass or fail grade. Swarthmore and Kenyon Colleges use outside examiners, thereby assuring better team effort between teacher and student.

The Cost

Undoubtedly some programs have been initiated with some hope of reducing cost. No reports were found showing that costs could actually be reduced, unless a major deficiency in the program accompanied the reduced cost. All of the programs reported by the Wooster study[11] show extra costs of some kind, but most institutions did not have the elaborate bookkeeping that could accurately determine the cost above course instruction. The investigators estimated that the maximum cost for any of the twenty programs was a twenty-five percent increase in instructional costs.

Also generally reported was that the initial costs in developing a program were higher because of waste motion, extra work required for new outlines and procedures, and greater demand for more books, more study space, and more materials. No matter how much was added, shortages were always felt.

Elementary and secondary schools will face equally large problems as they go through with the building changes required, with the faculty learning to repace themselves, and with the extra materials needed to encourage student explorations. However, as a guideline the cost need not exceed the capital needed to extend the nine-month school year to eleven months. With good management, the cost can be less.

Results

As experience has been gained in the use of independent study, certain recommendations keep reoccurring. While these cannot be considered as rigorous analyses by which to evaluate their effectiveness, the recommendations serve as feedback in reconstructing what might be tightly knit experimental programs.

While not indicating exactly how the conclusions were reached, Congreve reported that children in a laboratory school, working independently, learned as much content as other students, grew in ability to define and solve problems, and reordered their conceptions about the role of the teacher.[12]

An earlier survey by Hatch and Bennett indicated that honors programs have been broadened as the participants discovered that:

1. Grade points were often poor predictors of success;
2. Not all superior students are interested;
3. Upperclassmen often are poorly prepared because their work lacked breadth or depth;
4. The early passive learning roles made honors work distasteful.[13]

In a survey in 1964 Chickering asked teachers to pick five students as their ideal for independent work. He then asked them to describe these students. No unitary trait evolved. They saw these students as interdependent (relates to others but not dependent on them), venturesome or open to experience, resourceful, persistent, and reflective. He then more formally tested some hypotheses and found by outside measures that these students were more self-confident, more original, more theoretically oriented and had more aesthetic interests. They were lower on emotional disturbance and deviate thinking. No significant differences were found in intelligence, information, and academic skills.[14] He said that,

> ... measures of intellective factors do not [sic] discriminate whereas those of non-intellective factors do. ... In the study reported here, the distinguishing characteristics of successful independent students are ... social, emotional and attitudinal.[15]

The Wooster group has given the most complete picture through interviews about the reactions of students and faculty. The following excerpt uses the values that two hundred twenty-nine students and two hundred twenty-nine faculty advisors saw in the twenty college programs studied.[16]

Value	Students	Faculty
Develops ability to work resourcefully	99	80
Gives chance to probe intensively into special, personal interest	62	31
Teaches research techniques	58	64
Allows exploration in major field	52	45
Gives training in organization and presentation of material	48	50
Gives preparation for graduate work	37	42
"Six other values were listed"		

Faculty also indicated that they gained by independent study programs, mentioning such items as broadening one's own knowledge, creating closer student-faculty relationships, obtaining satisfaction in helping students develop competence, and aiding one's own research. However, they mentioned such drawbacks as demands on time and frustration with disinterested students.

The drawbacks for students, as seen by both students and faculty, included lack of guidance by advisors, procrastination, less demanding and rewarding satisfaction than course work, too little time and credit, limited facilities, and some other drawbacks, most of which dealt with program implementations and not with the basic nature of the independent study itself. Seventy percent of the students indicated they would take independent study if they were to do it over again.

In a study conducted at Sterling Morton High School in Cicero, Illinois (1960-61), a five-year follow-up was made of students who had an honors course in their senior year in mathematics. When comparing the honors students to a control population, no significant differences were found in grades received in college or in other factors thought important in the follow-up. There was one important exception. Twice as many of the honors group went into mathematics or math-related fields as did the control population.

Criteria for Planning Independent Study Programs

What independent study should consist of is difficult to answer. It is certainly not satisfactory to accept the prevailing practice as the ideal toward which a school might strive. The criteria for acceptable models should include internal consistency, adjustment for individual differences, expectations of the teacher's role and student activity, comprehensiveness, and outcomes.

Most programs have simply evolved out of the give-and-take of teachers and administrators as they wrestled with the practical problems of implementing an idea. The parallel to the farmer growing corn a century ago is striking. Then a farmer relied on common-sense knowledge, derived from immediate experiences and communicated primarily by word of mouth. He understood certain more obvious cause-and-effect relationships. He knew moisture and warmth were required. He had sufficient knowledge to produce what appeared to him were fairly high yields. He could even vaguely understand some failures such as those caused by disease. There was a definite plateau in the yield, however, which he did not know how to exceed. Furthermore, it probably did not even occur to him that the present yields of corn were anything but fantasy. But research that went beyond his common-sense experience soon caused various breakthroughs, two of these were hybrid seed corn and mineral fertilizers.

In the same fashion we now plan much of our education programs. We operate pretty well as the farmer did a century ago with his corn. We have enough common-sense knowledge about learning and education to produce our first plateau, but not much more.

To get beyond the first plateau will require us to put together programs of sufficient depth, concentration, and uniqueness to produce the chance of a major breakthrough. In doing this, there is need to utilize available research to suggest the possible nature of the uniqueness and to provide the framework for internal consistency. Thus, if independent study calls for maximizing student interest in an area, then his emotional satisfactions should come from the work itself and not from the extrinsic rewards of grades.

Adjustment for Individual Differences

Writing about individual differences, Shane has given a list of school objectives and practices that can be reflected in independent study. Independent study will not accomplish all of the goals of individualized instruction, but it should accomplish a number of them. Note how the items on the list (only partially listed and paraphrased here) fit the internal consistency criterion:

1. The organization should require varied rates of pupil progress.
2. Reporting should convey a clear idea of the pupil's rate of progress with respect to his particular developmental characteristics, such as potential, motivation, social relationships, mental health, and academic performance.
3. Subject matter must have meaning for the learner.
4. Administrative policies should be based on a continuum of cumulative experience.

The remaining items on his list are equally consistent.[17]

The Expectations of the Teacher's Role and Student Activity

Elementary and secondary schools will have to give greater heed than colleges to the nature of the student-teacher-materials relationship. The student is less mature. Less reliance can be placed on sink-or-swim tactics. Just as we tritely say that students must learn how to study, students must have assistance in choosing areas of study, in carrying on self-sustained activity, and in relating and integrating their experiences and readings. What to us may seem to be little freedom, may to them be confusion. Continuous assessment of the pupil-teacher relationship should be undertaken by both the pupil and the teacher. This is a new undertaking for a classroom teacher who seldom explores with a pupil the nature of the relationship between the two. Independent study makes this possible, both through individual conferences and small-group meetings.

Comprehensiveness

This criterion is suggested in light of the need to make any new approach comprehensive enough so that there is realistic expectation for measurable outcomes. Hatch and Bennett have suggested that we need an experimental program not made up of discrete courses but of integrated curriculum. They recommend that students be required to take all of their work in independent study for at least a semester and preferably for one or two years.

> An exposure of students to independent study for only three hours in fifteen, thirty, or even one hundred twenty, makes it difficult if not impossible to measure gains in critical thinking, creativity, or changes in attitudes and values. . . . Until more of a student's time is spent in what for him is a strange experience, we are not likely to learn whether independent study does or does not have the "plus values" predicted for it.[18]

In addition, they argue that other logical provisions be incorporated, such as early entrance into college, advanced placement, credit by examination, and comprehensive examinations. They state that this should be the ultimate in experimental synthesis.

Such a comprehensive approach has been called a *saturation* design which increases the likelihood of a measurable outcome. Once a measurable outcome has been determined, then various elements or ingredients can be removed, transposed, or replaced to determine empirically the internal consistency of the program. It must be quite evident that verbal descriptions, such as those in this book or in lectures or at conferences, do not in any way adequately describe or communicate what really goes on in independent study. Hatch and Bennett suggest that transcripts might be made of lectures, conferences, seminars, and colloquia, that lists be prepared of sources and readings used, and that syllabi be developed in diverse subjects to illustrate what has been done in independent study programs.

Outcomes

Few would argue that information retention is the most important outcome of independent study, but most would happily accept it as a by-product. The danger is that the desire for information retention will subtly creep into the expectations expressed by the teacher in the individual contacts with students or in small group meetings. Constant feedback from the students and other teachers in observation will make visible the more subtle expectations.

Certain growth outcomes should be expected. Examples of tangible measures are these:

1. The student undertakes a project with less teacher guidance.
2. The projects relate to two or more subject areas.
3. The student moves from the more passive role of reading to an active role of seeking out data by experimentation and interviews, and of moving out of the learning centers, laboratory, or carrels.
4. Interaction with other students shows less socializing and more task-oriented conversation.
5. Students make less demands for grades.

Each of these measures should be kept for individual students so that he can gauge his own progress. The more commonly used measures of academic work, socialization, motivation, and emotional health should also continue.

Demonstration Models

Brickell has shown that major educational changes, beyond those that an individual teacher can do in her own classroom, are most likely to follow a visit to a school where the program is actually being carried out. Certain conditions influence the visitor. First, the visitor must sense that the school he is visiting is similar to his own. Anything markedly unusual about the student population, the source of finances, or other features will cause him to reject what he has seen. Second, he is more concerned about what students have to say about the experience than the teachers or the administrators who, he understandably believes, may try to sell the program rather than simply to demonstrate it.[19]

Of course, someone must make up the first demonstration program by reading books such as this, reviewing research literature, and following their own intuitive hunches. As demonstrations might be a major source of change in public schools, outside agencies ought to give financial support and leadership to typical elementary and secondary schools in order to develop more visible, believable, and well-integrated demonstration programs. There is justification in elaborating such programs in greater detail than would be true if the school were left to its own financial resources for the initial planning and the implementation phases. Retooling costs are quite high. In helping schools develop their programs for talented and gifted children, the demonstration approach is now being tried by the State of Illinois with support from the United States Office of Education.

In addition to the working models in colleges and schools there are those recommended by persons such as Trump and Baynham.[20] In the March-April, 1963, issue of *The Superior Student* the major features of a full honors program—revisions of an earlier set of suggestions—were recommended. The revisions reflect a desire for more complexity and enriching provisions in honors work in contrast to the earlier models. The writers note that the outline is more explicit in asking credit for honors work and is less demanding of grades. Encouragement is given for inclusion of high school students, for students doing work abroad, for full-time professional counselors for honors work, for more explicit recognition of intuitive factors and cognition, and for more varied exploitation of research opportunities. The outline calls for more articulation between grade and organizational levels. Unfortunately, certain emphases in the total proposal either show ignorance of some research findings or simply reflect a highly selected interest in certain students. Thus, there is continual emphasis on high ability students and the grouping or isolating of these students from the rest of the student body. Not all of the sixteen features listed, of course, deal with independent study and its point of view. There is also emphasis on more structured work, especially as one moves into preprofessional and professional training. Yet many of the things not called independent study in the proposal nonetheless support the idea of making the student more self-directed in his work in the university.

The models that have been recommended by the National Association of Secondary School Principals are probably familiar enough to most readers.[21] Three such programs at the high school level in Illinois have now become part of the Illinois Demonstration Program for Gifted Children. These are Lakeview High School in Decatur, Ridgewood High School in Norridge, and Evanston Township High

School. However, much remains to be done in each of these schools to make more clearly visible to visitors what independent study consists of and might consist of in a high school setting.

A 1962 investigation of independent study by Huffmire gave examples of degrees of independent study reflected in practical projects undertaken by a single student or a group of students in science. Lowest on the order of continuum was "a problem work group" which primarily spent its time in confirming a known principle. Next were special reports that summarized the reading a student had done. This is similar to how most independent study programs begin in the colleges. He considered the best example of independent study to be a "problem solving group" where students dealt with problems suggested by research, ideas borrowed from historical science, or ideas suggested by the science teacher himself.[22]

Who Is to be Involved?

The proper answer is that all students in a particular school should be involved in independent study once the operational procedures have been worked out in a pilot program. The real problem is not to decide who shall be included or excluded in the program, but to determine what kinds of adjustment must be made for individual students so that all can be reached and properly challenged. We have been speaking for decades of providing for individual differences in the classroom without giving the teacher either proper assistance, enough time, or adequate training to do the task satisfactorily.

A team effort is required to make practical and sustained adjustments in the curriculum in light of what we know about each youngster. Understanding must be followed by planned action. Not often realized, the goal of providing for individual differences must develop an understanding of the student's personality and a knowledge about individual teachers and about whom they can relate with most satisfactorily. We need to work hard at matching youngsters with teachers. Such self-study by teachers means that they must be open to the idea of discovering which youngsters they relate with most satisfactorily and why. This in turn will require an administrative group whom the teachers will trust with such assessment.

One possible approach of mutual assessment would be to follow

the leads of the research produced by Chickering.[23] Such characteristics like interdependence, venturesomeness, curiosity, resourcefulness, persistence, and reflective behavior are the traits in which
growth ought to be observed. The teacher needs to find out which
characteristics she demonstrates in her own teaching behavior. Students should learn what is expected of them by being able to follow
the model set by their advisor.

Organization

Many kinds of organizational schemes will support an independent
study program, though all such organizational apparatuses must provide for in-service training. This is discussed in Chapter Eleven of this
book and touched on later in the chapter.

Some kind of team teaching or cooperative interaction is essential
in order to support the in-service training aspects of the program
and to bring in professional consultants like psychologists and
counselors. Unfortunately, the teaching profession is a highly isolated
profession. There is little chance for one teacher to see another in
action. Most of the communication must take place secondhand,
either by the teacher reporting her perceptions of her own teaching
or through a third person such as the principal or a curriculum
supervisor.

Cumulative folders best illustrate the organizational provision for
individual differences. Unfortunately, they are typically used to serve
the needs of the administration or of the teachers who in a sense are
to sit in judgment upon the student. Seldom are cumulative folders
viewed as the private property of the individual. Seldom are they
adequately used in the true educational sense of helping the individual to obtain a more adequate self-image. If, in the judgment of
any of the school staff, there is information about the youngster which
he is not yet ready to incorporate into a self-image, then the task of
the professional staff is not to withhold forever such information
from him, but to find ways and means for him to incorporate it
adequately. Almost inevitably the information that we do withhold
will be in other ways less adequately communicated to the person. If
he is not liked by other members of the class, he already knows this
by subtle or open rejection. If he has a low score on the aptitude
tests, he already can guess the score fairly well by the many com-

parisons he goes through in the grading procedures. If he comes from a lower socioeconomic level, he is quite aware, perhaps painfully aware, of what he wished he had that he observed his friends do have.

The organization must not isolate independent study activities from the rest of the school day, though the immediate problem is to differentiate independent study out of its too prevalent use as a study hall assignment. Because of the experiences of college faculty, schools seem best advised to integrate small-group discussions and independent work. The students can learn in small groups from the teacher what is expected of them in independent study. The students can share their experiences with each other.

Leuba[24] has described what appeared to be effective use of small groups in independent study. The approach makes sense because learning is reinforced through the social motives of the youngsters who want to gain attention and win approval by the performance of an academic task. Groups also provide immediate feedback to the student of his perceptions as he discusses them with his peers. The use of small groups is not a laissez-faire undertaking. Small-group activity must be given leadership by the instructor: first, as a consultant to help the group process, and, second, as a resource person who suggests means for students to accomplish their goals. Leuba has demonstrated small groups in front of a larger class in order to acquaint the students more adequately with what the activities of the group should consist.

In-Service Training

An independent study program that does not include an integrated in-service training program will not mature and meet the potential that otherwise might be possible. One essential for in-service training is feedback. Success or failure of an independent study program will depend on what occurs in the individual and group conferences involving the teacher, other professionals, and the students. Consequently, the conferences should be subjected to the closest scrutiny by the staff. The scrutiny can be done through tape recordings, team teaching effort, observation, and even video tape. Every possible measure of the interaction ought to be used to communicate to the participants and to the observers exactly what is going on. Several protocols or frameworks for analyses are available. One framework might involve the cognitive behavior by students. Even an inadequately conceived program can succeed if teachers begin to assess themselves and recognize within their own group some highly successful examples or demonstrations of what independent study might consist of.

Also, released time is important since the teacher will not be able to carry a full work load during the day and then on his own or an overtime basis do what is required for an adequate job of self-examination in a new program. If the administration recognizes self-assessment as part of the teacher's regular work load, not only is he being told it is important work to do, but also he receives powerful reinforcement that he is to devise a new *modus operandi* for himself. Admittedly, such an approach adds to the initial costs of the program. School districts might as well be frank with themselves and recognize that little can be accomplished in major overhaul of curriculum without this added expense. However, funds are becoming increasingly available from outside agencies to support such program development.

The teacher must have the trust of the administration as well as time to develop his self-assessment. Little can be hoped for even with adequate released time if the teachers do not feel they can trust the supervisor or administrator with the exposure of themselves as tape recordings are listened to, as students tell teachers what they see them doing, and as one teacher reacts to what another has undertaken. Such exposure demands an understanding and supportive atmosphere. Information revealed through such procedures must never enter into consideration of job advancements, merit pay, or other decisions that evaluate one teacher against another. A teacher has no choice but to be defensive and to play it safe with self-assessment procedures unless he can trust the persons with whom he is dealing.

A quick way for an administrator to find out whether he really can produce change, meaningful change, in the relationships between students and teachers is simply to ask for an anonymous response from his faculty as to whether he can be trusted with such information about the teacher which is gained from student assessment, tape recordings, and colleague reactions.

Although feedback implies study of the teacher's behavior by the teacher, a study of the youngsters is also necessary through various approaches. A start can be made with the information put into cumulative folders but always with the expectation that some kind of follow-up will be made. A standing question should be, "What action is to be taken in light of the understanding we have acquired about the student?" Independent study will take on its deepest meaning as understandings of students are incorporated into the planning conferences of teachers and students.

An in-service training program adequately conceived has almost all of the required elements for evaluation built into the procedures. The same measures of student and teacher assessment used for understanding the students and the interaction within the conferences can be used to assess growth both in the staff and in the students.

In addition, the products of the student need more careful analysis within some standardized framework other than the subjective judgments of instructors deciding whether a product deserves an A or B, or pass or fail. Such grading does not make clear on what basis the evaluation was made and serves no diagnostic function. If these measurements are reported in the literature, then independent study will become a more thoroughly understood curriculum program and more adequately judged on its merits as an educational tool.

Summary

Independent study is an established undergraduate teaching method in many colleges and universities. The student is given freedom from many or most of the usual requirements associated with course work, and he is expected to choose an area for study, to develop his own approach, and to produce some kind of outcome, such as a paper, an oral presentation, or a product.

Elementary and secondary schools are now exploring and building trial programs in independent study as a means of providing more adequately for individual differences. It appears that the efforts will succeed if in-service training can be incorporated into the plans. But the in-service program must scrutinize and build upon the heart of the process, the teacher-student small-group relationship, through intensive self-assessment procedures such as tape recordings, cumulative folders, and analysis of the products of the independent study.

CHAPTER 3

The University of Chicago Project

by

WILLARD J. CONGREVE

For the last three years Willard J. Congreve, principal of The University of Chicago Laboratory School, has been working with its staff in the development of its Freshman Project, which includes independent study. He received his master's degree from Northwestern University and his doctorate from the University of Chicago.

THE PROGRAM which I am about to describe, its evolution and its current status, must be viewed by the reader as incomplete. Although explicit attempts to develop independence among the students at The University of Chicago Laboratory High School have been underway for almost three years, conclusions reached at this point are tentative and must await further data for validation and clarification. It is even difficult, if not impossible, to view this program in proper perspective. Describing it at this time is like entering one side of a dense forest and attempting to describe the entire forest after viewing only a part of it.

We still have a long way to go before we will be ready to make a final report. However, I feel that a description of our efforts thus far may be valuable, so long as the account is interpreted as simply a summary of an on-going effort at a point in time.

I shall attempt to be candid—to describe our problems and even to relate our misgivings. Perhaps others who decide on a similar venture will be able to avoid our mistakes by analyzing the weaknesses portrayed in this description.

Credit for this effort goes to those members of our faculty who have pushed forward in the face of perplexing questions and skeptical colleagues. Whatever support was offered by the administration is dwarfed when compared to the immense contribution of time, talent, and fortitude of each project teacher.

Teachers Initiate Action

Development of the self-generating student—the student who knows how to know and takes responsibility for his learning—has long been an implicit goal of The University of Chicago Laboratory Schools. Seemingly without outside cues, teachers have for decades responded to the quality of the students assembled in this institution by attempting to place upon their shoulders the responsibility for analytical analysis and investigation in depth. However, up until 1961, from the description of the school's program of studies and schedule there was little to indicate that such a goal existed. To be sure, even though each teacher felt the urgency to prepare the students for the time when they would be continuing their studies in college on a semi-independent (if not independent) basis, the organizational structure of the school hampered the teachers in bringing this goal to fruition. Students were assigned into class groups of twenty to twenty-five per class, and classes met regularly four days a week. Students were expected to attend all class sessions. More than that, teachers were not even permitted to release students from class for independent work on any basis but a single student basis, for it was feared that free-roaming students would cause trouble.

During the school year 1960-61 two teachers[1] became restless with this situation. They felt that changes in the school structure could be made which would open up opportunities for the teachers to pursue the cherished goal of developing the student who knows how to know and applies this knowledge in pursuing learning on his own.

These two teachers proposed a pilot project in which students in World Geography and Earth Science would be scheduled together in a block of three periods (one period for each subject and a third for study use). The two teachers would work with these students, helping them identify problem areas and then turning them loose to pursue solutions on their own. Except for the obligation of the students to be in the project area (a four-room suite with folding doors) during the three periods (or working in the library), there would be no requirement to attend class sessions conducted by the teacher other than one large-group session per week in each subject area. In this session the teacher would help the students focus on problems and give them guidance in methods of approaching new problems. From that point on the work was to be directed mainly by the individual students. Papers and reports were to be submitted by the students to give evidence of their progress. Teachers and students could get together the remaining periods of the week in optional activities, initiated by the students or the teachers.

Pilot Project Results Encouraging

Because the pilot project was clinical—really a study to see what would happen to students under these circumstances—experimental controls could not be established. However, the pilot students were given the same post-tests at the end of the school year as were the nonpilot students. Actually, the pilot group gained as much in subject matter mastery as did the nonpilot group in spite of the remarkably short period of time spent in formal class sessions. Furthermore, after the students got over the joy and shock of not being told what to do every minute, they tended to settle down and work quite well without the need for formal sessions. To be sure, "goofing off" was evident —perhaps more evident than in a regular classroom setting. One must realize that when students are in a formal classroom situation, their lack of attention is more difficult to perceive than when they are free as a group to do as they wish. It is guessed that the amount of time wasted among the pilot group was in reality no more than that wasted by the regular classroom group.

Other interesting results appeared. Some students became so engrossed in projects that they wrote fifty to seventy-five reports on their findings—a feat unheard of among the regular classroom group. Furthermore, the students seemed to find a new use for the teacher. Often a small group would request that the teacher meet with them to discuss problem implications or to get assistance which they could not obtain in any other way. They found the teacher a compatible partner in the learning process, using him as a resource at the most opportune times.

In spite of the tremendous amount of freedom extended to these students, the roof of the school building did not collapse; the students did not destroy their classrooms; and learning proceeded in an amazingly orderly manner.

Project Expanded for Second Year

If such a project was possible with forty-two students, why not involve the entire freshman class of one hundred seventy-five students and extend the program to four subjects (English, science, social studies, and mathematics)? This question seemed plausible at least to the principal and to the project faculty. However, it was difficult to locate eight teachers with the same commitment as that held by Bernstein and Poll. We did succeed in locating two more who were willing to attempt to work together in some kind of flexible framework. Using these as a core, we built our group of eight by assigning to the project four new teachers who were being added to the faculty. The project faculty was then employed for four weeks during the summer to meet together and work out plans for the coming year. The only instruction given them by the administration was that they were to develop a program in which students would learn how to learn, in which they would gain the skills and insights that would enable them to pursue knowledge in a block of time, and the teachers were free to develop whatever structure seemed best to them.

Coming to a decision about the structure of this project was not an easy matter. When the eight teachers sat down around the table, they found little difficulty in agreeing upon the basic principles of the project and were willing to accept the intrinsic value of the goal of student independence. However, the means which were to be used to achieve this goal were not so readily agreed upon. Some teachers felt that the only way a student could learn how to learn in their subject was to check daily with the teacher on his progress. Progress was viewed as a step-by-step process through a preconceived body of knowledge, all steps having been carefully worked out according to principles of sound learning theory. Others felt that students could leapfrog through their subject, taking up problems of varying difficulty, disregarding the usual learning sequence. They felt sure that as students were confronted in problem situations with needs for skills or content, time could then be taken for them to learn these materials. Faculty opinion as to how much freedom could be allowed to the students as they pursued learning in the four subject areas ranged from absolutely no time taken from the regular class periods to no more than one regular class meeting per week. Interestingly enough, the opinion tended to differ subject by subject— mathematics and English feeling that more regular class time was needed, while science and social studies seemed content with less class time. However, rather wide differences of opinion also existed between the two teachers in each subject area.

Most of the teachers agreed, however, that if students were to learn what it means to work on one's own and to take responsibility for one's learning, they must have some learning experiences which required them to proceed on their own deciding what they were going to do, ordering a portion of their time, and taking responsibility for the consequences of their decisions.

Student Options Accepted as Essential Ingredient

Finally, a compromise starting structure was agreed upon by the teachers. The classes would all meet regularly three periods a week, and the remaining two periods (or two full days) would be reserved for optional learning activities. The teachers would develop plans for the option days which would be presented to the students on Friday of each preceding week. The option choices would include a wide variety of activities. Independent study in the library, discussion sessions in a group study room, student-led discussions, teacher-led discussions, remedial work on study skills and basic fundamentals, teacher lectures, laboratory work, and audiovisual activities were among the choices to be offered for all four subjects. As each student determined his own program of activities for his eight free option periods for the coming week, he would be able to elect from over forty different activities combinations.

Numerous pretests were administered to the students during the first week. These tests included subject-matter achievement tests, the Watson-Glaser Assessment of Critical Thinking, attitude measure, and some personality measures. During the second week the students were assigned into teachable groups by the project faculty and were oriented to the option program. Most of the students plunged into the idea with vigor. However, not too many weeks passed before it became apparent that some students just could not bring themselves to use the option days in a manner conducive to learning. They went to *silent study* not really expecting to work silently. Group study options sometimes became boisterous discussion sessions on topics entirely unrelated to the curriculum. The library was a place to do nothing but read current popular magazines or to listen to favorite popular musical recordings.

Although this response on the part of some students was to be expected, it was disheartening to some of the project faculty. Those who agreed to the option plan with reservations used this kind of student response as evidence that the group had made an unwise decision. Even though a large majority of the students appeared to be using their time wisely, the rather significant number of non-directed students caused great concern.

Teachers Modify Starting Plan

After two marking periods had passed and after some students, in spite of low achievement, still found it impossible to elect what was helpful to them or to stick to useful choices once made, it became apparent that the program selected at the beginning was not the best one for all students. The question then loomed: "What could be done for the students who needed more structure and guidance on a regular basis from the faculty, without interfering with the marvelous progress being made by the others under the three-day-class two-day-option program?" Furthermore, could the independent dimension of the program be extended to provide even more freedom for a smaller group of students, who were obviously being hampered in their learning by being required to attend class sessions even three days a week?

The creative project faculty put their minds to work and came up with a remarkably flexible plan. Three program types would be offered to the students. Type I would be defined as a kind of return to tradition, with four or five class sessions per week which would be essentially teacher-directed and teacher-planned. Type II would con-

tinue the three-day-class two-day-option program as originally outlined, and Type III would involve only one required class meeting
per week (more on demand of the students) and would be essentially student-planned and student-directed. It was agreed that, in
keeping with the goal of developing within each student the ability
to decide what was best for him, the faculty would offer the three
type choices to the students and after some discussion and elabora-
tion, each student would be free to select his program. Also, because
this was to be a new experience, no student would be bound to his
first choice for more than six weeks. However, after two six-week
trial periods, the student would be required to make a final choice at
the beginning of the third quarter which he would use for the remainder of the year.

Different choices were permitted for each of the four subjects.
However, scheduling problems did make it difficult to give each
student the full range of choices indicated. Interestingly, about
twenty percent of the students elected Type I and about twenty
per cent elected Type III. The majority of the students (sixty percent) chose to remain in Type II. There were a surprisingly small
number of pure types; that is, students who elected the same type in
all four subjects. Some changes were effected at the reelection periods. However, about ninety percent of the students kept the same type
plan for the balance of the year.

The three-type plan seemed to solve the major problem of limited
opportunities for some students which existed in the single three-day-
class two-day-option plan; therefore, the program continued under
the new plan for the remainder of the year. But the new program did
not eliminate all the problems. Development of good options which
students felt were interesting as well as useful plagued the faculty.
Options which the teachers considered excellent learning opportunities often were not popular with the students. And fun-type
options, movies and the like, tended to aggravate some of the faculty
of the University School.

Other University School staff energy was directed toward developing administrative systems for keeping track of the students as they
moved through the option program. Although not perfected until
the second year's full program, an IBM attendance system was developed which facilitated the recording of students' whereabouts

without interfering with student freedom to move about. The final plan, as is presently in use, will be discussed in the section on the current year's program.

Data from Expanded Program also Promising

Unfortunately, data from the first year of the expanded study could not be completely collected and subsequently processed until the second year was well underway. However, the results, as they are now becoming available, do present promising indications which warrant continuing the project even beyond its second full year. The data also are raising challenging questions which must be eventually answered if our efforts are even to lead to a program which can be depended upon to reach the desired goals for a majority of the students involved.

Data was collected from five sources: pre- and post-teacher-made subject-matter tests; pre- and post-standardized tests; a questionnaire administered to the parents at the same time as one administered to the students, and a questionnaire administered to the sophomore teachers of the project students after they had worked with the students for three months as sophomores.

Although the pre- and post-test data and the comments of the sophomore faculty members reinforced the findings from the pilot project that the students had learned as much subject matter as had other freshman students in the past, other data, especially when related to the level of independence which the student elected during the freshman project, provided some rather surprising but not entirely unexpected results.

Aptitude and Achievement Related to Independence

Early in the program the freshman teachers commented that it appeared that the students were electing programs of dependence (Type I) or independence (Type II and III) on some bases other than ability or general achievement level. Teacher observations seemed to reveal that both the bright and not-so-bright students could be found in any of the three programs and that there did not seem to be any pattern of ability accompanying the selection made by the students. However, when the data were carefully analyzed at the close of the first year's full program, it was found without question that students who characteristically selected the more dependent (Type I) approach in one or more subjects differed significantly from those who characteristically selected the more independent (Type II or Type III) approach on practically every ability and achievement measure.

When the students were grouped into composite Type I, Type II, and Type III groups (that is, the final type selection which was made for the longest period of time and after the students had had an opportunity to determine which type seemed to be best suited to them), the difference among the three types became even clearer. It was apparent from the examination of these data that the students with the highest I.Q., the highest grade point averages, and the highest scores on the School College Aptitude Tests were found in the independent Type III programs, and those with the lowest I.Q., the lowest School College Aptitude Test scores, and the lowest grade point averages were found in the dependent Type I programs. The Type II group scores fell in between the Type I and Type III group scores and were significantly different from the other two groups.

Thus, it now appears that students who were the most capable (according to all ability and achievement measures presently available to us) sought out the most independent programs, and, according to the grade point averages achieved, did the best work. Students who, by all usual measures, were the weakest sought out the program which gave them the greatest amount of teacher contact; yet they got the lowest grades.

Other tests yet to be made on the data available involve some attempt to hold I.Q. and ability measures constant or to find comparable students in all three groups and determine whether or not achievement differs by the type chosen. However, at this writing the most that can honestly be said is that the highest achieving brightest students elected the programs which provided for the greatest student independence in determining methods of study.

Varied Student Reaction to Project

When the students were asked to respond to questionnaire items which attempted to assess their personal feelings about the project, their reactions to the freedom offered and to the opportunities for self-direction and independent learning ranged all the way from enthusiastic, wholehearted approval to utter disgust. Because the students were questioned as sophomores after they had returned to what could be described in our school as a normal program, they had the advantage of comparing the experimental freshman program with the sophomore program. When asked what kind of program they would like for their junior year, the group was split almost in half. Fifty-four percent requested a freshman type program and forty-six percent requested a sophomore type program. When their parents were asked the same question, a slight but not significant reversal occurred—forty-nine percent of those responding requested a freshman type program for their children and fifty-one percent requested a sophomore type program.

When given opportunities to comment freely on various phases of the program, the student responses ranged along the entire continuum from total support of the program to complete rejection. Some students felt that the program was too restrictive, others thought it was far too permissive. Some felt that the teachers did not give them enough opportunities to work on their own; others described the teachers as being entirely non-directive. A rather consistent criticism, however, was voiced by many of the students. They complained that the option program tended to lose its vigor as the year wore on; the offerings seemed to become stereotyped. Some students even concluded from what they perceived to be poorer quality options that faculty interest itself in the project waned during the year.

Other more encouraging responses were obtained from students. A majority of them said that the program provided them with an opportunity to learn more about themselves and how they studied. When asked, "Did the types provide you with more understanding about how you learn than you could have achieved in a regular program?" Sixty percent or more of the students responded favorably, citing specifically the dimensions of study habits, budgeting of time, finding the best or most appropriate materials, determining how one comes to decisions about what one will do and what one has to work hardest on. The students readily credited the *modus operandi* of the project which required them to make choices on their own as that factor which caused them to learn these things about themselves.

Students Note Outstanding Advantages

A few specific student anecdotes and unsolicited reactions were also encouraging. One student came to the principal after a year in the freshman project and asked to be relieved of his German class. He said that under the freshman type and option program he could elect to spend less time on mathematics and thereby have more time for German, the latter being the harder subject for him. But now that he had become a sophomore he no longer would have the opportunity to alter class time commitments. Therefore, because he could no longer give extra time to German, he felt it would be better to drop the subject than to risk an unsatisfactory grade. This student's grades of four A's in the freshman project subjects and a B in German confirm that he had indeed assessed his abilities accurately and could well afford less than the regular class time in the four required subjects.

Several students commented that the freshman year was the most exciting educational experience they had ever had. Others admonished the administration to put an end to this foolishness. Still others commented favorably on the project idea but reflected that they had done rather badly because they had not taken full advantage of the opportunities offered. Several students questioned the wisdom of having the project at such a young and tender age and suggested that they would be able to profit much more from such an opportunity as juniors and seniors; they felt it would get them ready for college.

Summary of First Year's Expanded Program

In summary, data from the first year of the full project seem to suggest the following:

1. Students with the highest achievement and greatest ability elect programs which permit them to work more on their own, while students with the lowest achievement and ability elect programs which provide them more direct guidance by the teacher. Until some better ways of defining and measuring behaviors related to independence in the various subject-matter fields are developed, we cannot seem

to separate, at least from our experience, students who thrive under an atmosphere of so-called independence from those who have high intelligence or high capacity for learning academic subjects and who concomitantly achieve in school at a high level.

2. In spite of the long-held notion about teen-agers desiring freedom to work out their own destinies, when given the opportunity to plan their programs, to select modes of study and to take the consequences for these selections, only about half of the freshman students in a high ability student population really are comfortable with such a situation and wish to have it continue. A sizable percentage of them (about fifteen percent) are so uncomfortable with this situation that they react almost violently against the idea after having been subjected to it. On the other hand, a similar percentage (again about fifteen percent) are tremendously enthusiastic about the program and feel cheated when such opportunities are terminated.

3. There seems to be no relationship between the amount of class time students spend with a teacher and the amount they learn. Despite the fact that the Type III students had the most infrequent class meetings these students received the highest grades and made the greatest gains on pre- and post-test data. Of course, they were also the brightest students and therefore undoubtedly got the most out of the class experiences which they had with the teachers.

4. In addition, we discovered that even with one hundred seventy-five students, it was possible to organize and operate a program where students had a considerable amount of freedom and not have the school disintegrate for lack of order. We also discovered that teachers can work together in developing programs far more complicated than administrators have ordinarily dared to tackle and that when teachers do have complete control over the instructional process, they will find solutions to organizational problems which are closer to meeting the needs of the learning situation.

Again, the students did not suffer in their subject-matter mastery from this full-blown project. Furthermore, many students reported positively on the experience. However, the results were still inconclusive, and replication of the program during the second school year seemed essential.

The Full Project Begins Its Second Year

The second year of the project has proceeded essentially as did the first year of the project. After a two-week orientation and testing program, the students were all placed in a three-day class two-day option program for twelve weeks. This plan was decided upon to provide each student with an initial choice-making, consequence-taking experience. At the beginning of the winter quarter (after Christmas vacation) the students were offered choices among the three learning types. The choices were reviewed by the students twice during the winter quarter; and now, at this writing, students have just completed making their final selections for the spring term.

The second year of the program is much improved over the first year's venture. The student orientation was better; the expectation for choice-making was initiated more gradually; and the assignment of a fully qualified counselor has vastly improved the guidance functions. However, problems similar to those experienced during the first year of the program have again raised their ugly heads. It is still impossible to meet the demands of the student who would like to take Type I in one subject, Type II in another, and Type III in still others. Reports of students' wasting time and of those who cannot select useful options continue to pour in. Project faculty find these reports disconcerting and often take to questioning the wisdom of the whole idea.

However, the faculty has succeeded in developing a system of keeping track of the students as they move from option to option which seems to work well. This system also provides each student with an accurate, regular report on how he has spent his optional time. Using a prepunched IBM card, students assign themselves to options each Friday by punching appropriate holes in a personalized card. These cards (eight in all for each student) are then sent to our statistical laboratory where they are sorted by "option" and used for printing class lists for the teacher in charge of the option. By Monday morning a class list for each option is in the hands of the teacher. The IBM cards are then filed to be used later (about once every five weeks) for printing a summary of option choices for each student. This summary is given to the student at about the same time he receives grades for the regular marking period. Thus, a student can look at his option choices and his grades and supposedly come to some wise conclusions about whether or not he is using his option time effectively.

After the first ten weeks of the second-year program the present freshman group had spent thirty-five percent of its time in teacher-led discussions, twenty-seven percent of its time in the library, thirteen percent viewing audiovisual materials, seven percent in student-teacher conferences, six percent in student-led presentations, five percent in individual and group study, three percent in laboratory work, two percent in teacher lectures, and two percent in counseling activities. At the end of this year these data will be useful in identifying students who have been the most independent (occupied their time in activities which did not involve the teacher) and those who have been least independent, regardless of the type of class chosen. This further analysis is essential because it is quite possible for a student in a Type III class to elect all teacher-led discussion options on option days and thereby actually participate in what is essentially a five-day teacher-directed program, whereas a student in Type II can attend teacher-led discussions only during his three days of assigned classes and spend the other two days entirely in independent study situations.

New Problems Now Being Recognized

Although the mechanics of the second year seem far less complicated than those of the first year, other problems are now looming before the project faculty. The "how are we going to make this thing work" having been fairly well settled, the faculty now finds its attention focusing on problems involving individual students and are beginning to ask the more fundamental questions of "why are we really doing this" and "what is this thing called independence that we are seeking to develop?" Furthermore, the so-called flexible program is beginning to emerge as a complicated program with new kinds of inflexibility. Such fundamental questions as the following are now puzzling our project staff:

1. Can all the subjects be adapted in some way to incorporate pursuit of learning on one's own, or is progress in some subjects or parts

of subjects at this stage of learning dependent upon constant teacher direction and supervision?

2. When we give a student freedom to choose and he elects library or silent study which in effect may end up in his doing nothing, do we accept this doing nothing as permissible behavior in the framework of independence? If so, do we accept it indefinitely, or do we work to change this pattern of behavior?

3. Are we to accept as an inherent responsibility of the teachers in the project that of pushing the students along toward greater independence—that is, push the Type I's to becoming Type II's and the Type II's to becoming Type III's? Or do we leave this choice entirely up to the student, hoping that in time either his own intrinsic desire for freedom or peer pressure or other societal pressures will eventually force him to move out from under the dominance of the teacher?

4. Has method somehow overshadowed purpose? Do the teachers find themselves maintaining a system of class time and option time at the expense of directing their attention toward changes in student behavior and then altering the system to fit the current student development?

5. Does this behavior which we so readily call independence have something to do with higher mental processes as opposed to lower mental processes? Is it in effect a kind of problem-solving ability? Does it have some of the earmarks of creativity? Is it a function of personality and, as such, inextricably interlaced with motivation, values, interests, and attitudes? Is the *independent* student in effect an *interdependent* student, using whatever sources are available to learn as rapidly and efficiently as possible so that he can ultimately develop the kind of background which will make it possible for him to focus on problems and questions which have not been solved even by the experts?

Teachers Face Themselves as They Face the New Problems

These questions are currently causing alternate discouraging and exhilarating effects on the project faculty. The teachers are now coming to grips with the complicated aspects of learning and instruction for which there are no pre-set maps or reliable guidelines. Traditional procedures which have been thought valid are being questioned. Old established ideas do not die quickly or without a fight, and certainly they must not be scuttled without careful, objective scrutiny.

Teachers cannot help but be influenced by their own past experiences in learning their subject matter. Not one of them was really exposed, at least as high school students, to free-choice-making situations as they prepared themselves in their field for the teaching profession. They were subjected, as were most students in the past hundred years, to teacher-planned lessons, explicit assignments, textbook readings, and the usual carefully guided paths. They cannot help but ask themselves, "Have I been thwarted academically as a result of my educational experiences, or am I quite an acceptable scholar in my field?" If they are reasonably satisfied with their present development, then the logical conclusion for them to draw is: "Then why are we trying to upset what has already been proven for something which undoubtedly is causing considerable unrest among some of the students and some of the parents, as well as among ourselves?"

Frustration Leads to Further Progress

In view of the complexities which now beset us, what are our future plans for this program? In reality, the future looks far brighter than it appears on the surface.

Our findings, in balance, are encouraging, and our tampering with the lockstep organizational procedures has been successful. Furthermore, our entire faculty to a man all agree that secondary education should be doing more for students than simply filling them with information and concepts. Our teachers are ready to admit that outlining every step for the student, filling his head with information that can be regurgitated on an examination, permitting the student to maintain passive existence in the learning process are probably not conducive to his developing the ability to learn how to learn. They accept unhesitatingly the responsibility to help students learn how to learn. They are willing to concede that essentially the act of learning is an individualized matter. And attempting to teach a class of students as a group rather than as an aggregation of varied individuals is recognized as a false approach.

The frustrations and anxieties of the project faculty are being directed toward a creative search for new answers. Already our science staff, Ernest Poll and Lila Woodruff, has begun work with our research consultant, Richard Wolf, in defining behaviors which seem to be the essential ingredients in developing the skills and the impetus to carry on learning on one's own. These behaviors are being tested among the students in the present freshman science classes, and the testing will soon be expanded to other subject areas. It is anticipated that a set of "learning how to learn" behaviors common to several subjects can be identified and validated before the end of this school term.

When these behaviors are identified, then evaluative measures can be developed which we can use to identify the extent to which our students have developed these behaviors before they begin the freshman program, and the extent to which these behaviors are developed or enlarged upon as a result of the various kinds of learning experiences provided to the students as members of the project.

If the true dimensions of independence can be defined operationally for each subject area, and if at least some of these can be further generalized for all four subject areas, then one major source of conflict among the project faculty will be eliminated. All teachers will then feel confident that they know what they are trying to do, and all will understand how their subject matter fits into the overall program.

Several Alternative Plans Being Considered

The next major problem will then be to try to develop teaching-learning situations which are most conducive to the development or furtherance of these independent behaviors. This will undoubtedly lead to some conflict because each teacher, or at least teachers of the various subject-matter fields, will undoubtedly suggest methods which are somewhat different. We may find, for example that the commitment to the three-day-class two-day-option program cannot be continued for the entire project. We may have to search for either a new type of general format or agree to use two or more formats and then study the growth of the students as they participate in the various formats.

We have already begun considering different possibilities. One approach would be to have four teachers, one in each subject, work together as a subteam, and the other four teachers work together as a different subteam. Each subteam would develop its own format for working with the students assigned to it. The progress of the students could then be compared, subteam against subteam.

Another possibility would be to try to make arrangements for teachers to have complete freedom in the way in which they would work with the students in their respective classes. They could release some, all, or none of them at any time to self-study projects. Teachers could document the program in individual logs. This would involve some coordination and prior agreement about the use of various study areas; but under these circumstances the teachers could change their style and methods of working with a particular class at any time, depending upon the kinds of things under study and the level of "learning how to learn" development among the various members of the class.

A third possibility would be to test the students at the beginning of the year with the *learning how to learn* or independent measurement devices and then sort the students into classes by the level of growth already indicated. Then each teacher could proceed to work with each group in ways which he felt would enhance the further growth of these dimensions as well as contribute to growth in subject-matter mastery. Frequent retesting or other means of evaluating student growth could be done throughout the year, and the groups could be reshuffled periodically so that more students could be set to working more on their own as the year wore on.

A fourth possibility includes a consideration of some of the work which is being done in identifying different styles of teaching and learning on The University of Chicago campus. Several new models are presently in the formative stages of development by several eminent University of Chicago educators. These may be ready for field testing soon and might become the basis for developing specific ways of working with students or with different classes. For example, independence suggests varying degrees of freedom allowed to students as they proceed with learning tasks. Classes could be set up with preconceived definitions of freedom, depending upon the level of development of the students. Furthermore, independence also suggests varying levels of mental processes. Students who learn simply by answering questions to workbook problems or through teaching machine Skinnerian-type stimuli are working at one level of mental process, while the graduate doctoral candidate who, on his own, identifies an original problem for study and carries this problem through to completion is working at an entirely different level of mental process. Somehow, classes might be developed which could involve varying proportions of lower and higher mental process dimension expectations.

Faculty Commitment Essential

But our problems will not be totally solved with a better definition of independence and with some better knowledge of how we might proceed. Actually, assignment of the faculty members to the project in the future will have to be done very carefully. Some of our current conflict undoubtedly stems from lack of commitment among the faculty to the basic philosophical issues. Therefore, the first prerequisite for assignment to the project staff henceforth will be a commitment to the philosophy, definitions, and structure to be followed. To be sure, each teacher being considered for appointment to the project will have extensive opportunity for reviewing and discussing what the intentions of the commitment are, but commitment for one year to the program as finally defined will be essential. Once this commitment is established, the group leader or chairman can proceed with full confidence that all teachers are pulling toward the same end.

Definite statement of function, clear-cut understanding of procedure, a sound program of evaluation, and total faculty commitment are now seen as the vital ingredients to advancing our program to the level where it can make a substantial contribution to the educational field.

In this short discussion, I have attempted to describe the evolution of one program designed to help students develop independence. I have tried to be explicit about the program and also frank about its problems and its future. I have tried to point out that simply deciding to develop a program to enhance the development of independent behaviors in a student body and coming up with new ways to manipulate the environment which on the surface seem to be conducive to the development of independence constitute only the barest beginning. It is not long before the teacher becomes aware that environment manipulation and scheduling alterations by themselves do not necessarily lead to new student achievements. The teacher will probably come to this opinion long before the administrator does. In fact, after a short period of time, the better teachers will confront the bitter and difficult questions and will soon find themselves in a state of severe frustration unless arrangements are made to pursue these questions in scholarly fashion.

Suggestions to Other Schools

What does our experience at The University of Chicago Laboratory Schools suggest to other school administrators who are interested in developing instructional programs which will foster the development of student independent behaviors? Or, what does our experience say to those who are just interested in breaking the lockstep patterns to which schools have been held for such a long time?

I would hope that administrators and teachers would not be discouraged by our experiences. Although we have experienced considerable frustration, we now find ourselves most optimistic with regard to the future. Our frustration has goaded us toward continued and more perceptive action. We feel confident that the course we will soon decide upon will move us substantially towards finding new knowledge which will give us at least partial answers to the perplexing questions.

Our experience these past three years point to at least five suggestions to those who want to initiate change:

1. The first and most important suggestion is simply, "Start! Don't wait any longer!" The principal will undoubtedly be able to find some teachers who are discontented with the *status quo*. He should get them talking together about how they think the school ought to be changed. He can encourage them to begin working on some kind of proposed pilot program which they think will effect the changes. As soon as they have something which appears operational, *let them begin.*

2. The second suggestion hinges directly on the first. The principal should not insist that this teacher group develop a defensible written philosophy and a clear-cut set of goals before he lets them get underway. Even though most curriculum theorists suggest that goals and philosophy should be a part of every plan, I would suggest that the best way to ruin a good idea or to smother faculty excitement is to table the plan until the philosophy and goals are clearly defined. To be sure, at some later time this definition will be essential to further experimentation. (Our Freshman Project has now reached this stage.) But, initially, I strongly suggest that the principal let the program which the teachers outline infer the philosophy and the objectives. He must have some simple faith that his teachers' best hunches are valid and let it go at that.

3. My third suggestion is that time and funds be provided for teacher planning, if at all possible. If teachers are to be turned loose to think creatively, they are going to need time to do it. Summer is an excellent period for this kind of work. Teachers are relaxed and full of enthusiasm. Above all, teachers who are responsible for one hundred twenty-five to one hundred fifty students each day, who must meet five classes often requiring different preparations for at least two of them, cannot be expected to come to afternoon or evening planning meetings refreshed and creative. Ideas just do not come out of humans under these conditions. Once the project is underway, teachers can usually find some time and energy to plan during the year to keep it going. But the initial plans will rarely arise from teachers who are already giving more of themselves than is humanly defensible.

4. Once the project gets underway, the principal and other school administrators must support it and the teachers. One ready argument in support of any teacher-initiated project is the intensive commitment with which teachers enter into the program. Project teachers spend far more time than does the usual teacher in a traditional situation thinking about program development and cause-and-effect relationships. This reflection and intensive planning cannot help but increase the teacher's effectiveness with his students.

The principal should not worry about the effectiveness of teachers who involve themselves in special experimental programs or be overly concerned about the effect such a program might have on the students. It is a safe prediction that the end result is going to be as good as or better than the teacher would have achieved in a regular program.

5. After the program has become operational, the principal should begin talking with his project faculty about the more fundamental aspects of it. Questions should be raised which will cause the teachers to reflect upon the ultimate purposes and upon the design of the program. It should not be surprising to discover that the teachers already will have been asking themselves similar questions. Good teachers just will not be content to remain for long in the dabbling stage. The Hawthorne Effect will soon wear off, and they will want to zero in on the goals and work with evaluation and research design consultants to clarify and intensify their efforts toward the desired ends.

When this time arrives, the teachers should be provided with the support and assistance they need. Administrators should remember that most teachers have never been trained in effective evaluation techniques and virtually none have ever learned how to set up a research or experimental design. Therefore, when they have reached the point of defining their problem, teachers will need specialized assistance to refine the program.

Research Design Requires Flexibility

These five suggestions may seem peculiar to one steeped in the so-called scientific method. However, the procedures just outlined can, it seems to me, be defended in a scientific framework. During the first year the teachers will be exploring. They will be trying to put their hands on what is wrong and at the same time suggesting ways to do something about it. One good way to identify a problem is to begin treating symptoms and observing the results. Scientists do work in this way; they do fumble; they do make mistakes; and they do retrace their steps over and over again. Teachers must be allowed to proceed on their best hunches in the same way the scientist works. In time enough data will be gleaned so that hypotheses can be generated and a research structure established.

The program at The University of Chicago Laboratory Schools has now reached this stage of development. Its future depends upon whether we can define operationally the behaviors which we all sense are important to develop, whether we can find ways to evaluate growth in these behaviors, and finally whether we can create a situation which will permit us to carry out teaching-learning activities specifically designed to develop these behaviors. We know better now what we are looking for. I do not believe we could have arrived at this state without the exploratory years.

Experimental Schools Are Productive Schools

Of course, schools and administrators can elect to wait until programs such as are underway at The University of Chicago Laboratory Schools, the Melbourne High School, the Ridgewood High School, and others have run the entire gamut of experimental stages and have produced new defensible procedures. Then, like the students in the physics lab, these wait-and-see schools can copy the new developments. Certainly this is the economical way to proceed, but it does deprive both faculty and students of the excitement and personal satisfaction which comes from exploration. Moreover, a school which follows this plan runs the risk of never changing because no new program will ever exactly fit another school's needs.

One of the most exciting and significant findings which came out of the Eight-Year Study[2] was that which indicated that the students who came from the most highly experimental high schools were the most successful in college. This seems to suggest that something important happens to the learning atmosphere of a school when it becomes engaged in experimental programs. Since I believe that every school has the potential in its faculty and student body for inquiry activities, I strongly recommend that schools everywhere become engaged in creative investigation.

CHAPTER 4

Independent Study with Team Teaching

by
WILLIAM FROMM

As principal of Lakeview High School, Decatur, Illinois, William Fromm works with a staff that dedicates nearly a third of each student's day to independent study, a vital element of the Decatur-Lakeview Plan. Mr. Fromm, who received his master's degree from the University of Missouri, was formerly the assistant principal of Centennial Junior High School in Decatur.

INDEPENDENT STUDY offers its greatest promise when it is part of a program which utilizes team teaching and has a flexible schedule. In such a program, independent study takes its place beside large-group and small-group instruction as at least an equal partner in the educational process.

Thelen points out that the process of education is a natural process and "that life is a continual natural inquiry into ways of resolving the conflict in each of its confrontations." He goes on to suggest that "the task of education is to supervise this natural inquiry and the educative process."[1] Thelen, therefore, identifies as most crucial a phase of the learning process that is generally ignored in the schools —Independent Study.

The purpose of the independent study program is to tear down the barriers to human inquiry that exist even in institutions geared for education. It has been said that education is growth, more growth, and even more growth. A school organized for independent study provides the students with guidance, facilities, materials, resource people, and various types of evaluation in areas of inquiry of the students' choice. Students in every school at one time or another encounter conflicts or concerns that call for further investigation, but too often the lack of time, resources, or freedom discourage further study. The independent study program is intended to remove these barriers to the search for knowledge.

The first step that must be taken before introducing a program of independent study into a school is the development of a working definition that fits the individual school situation. The definition must be broad enough to include all types of study that take place without direct supervision, but it must make distinctions between homework, teacher-assigned projects, and student-assumed work. At Lakeview Junior-Senior High School confusion was eliminated by dividing the program into three levels and naming each level.

This is the program:

Level One: Independent Study

Independent study involves student-assumed assignments which may grow from the regular course of study but are usually outside or beyond the regular curriculum. This work may or may not be graded. Its purpose may range from student interest to college credit.

Independent study involves students who have the ambition and desire to learn for the sake of learning. They may often be the highly capable or gifted students, but any student with sufficient interest may have the opportunity to work on his own independent study project.

Typical projects:

1. Latin American history in Spanish—Spanish.
2. Modern Mathematics by programmed learning—eighth grade Mathematics.
3. The industries of Japan—Social Studies.
4. Determining the orbit of spacecraft—Mathematics.
5. A study in depth of the *Canterbury Tales*—English.

Level Two: Individual Study

Individual study is teacher directed. The primary difference between these assignments and typical homework is that individual assignments are open-ended, giving a student an opportunity to go as far as he desires even though he is working under the guidance of a teacher.

Students from all achievement levels do individual assignments as a part of their regular course work. The difficulty of the assignments cover a wide range dependent upon the ability of the student. Course credit is usually given for this work. The projects often give rise to independent study projects.

Typical projects are:

1. Term papers—all curricular areas.
2. Collection and identification of minerals—Science.
3. A study of the life of Archimedes—Mathematics.
4. Overhauling a lawn mower engine—Power Mechanics.
5. Preparing a solo for a contest—Music.

Level Three: Homework

These assignments are specific, teacher-made, and have definite goals. They may be sentences to diagram, problems to work, or any of the necessary types of drill work. They may be done in study hall, in the instructional materials center, or at home.

This definition or description of the study program has served its purpose well because it has placed every student and his work within the study program. Each pupil participates at each level, but since every assignment falls some place on the independent study continuum, any extra effort or initiative by the teacher or student will move him closer to the opportunities offered by the highest level of independent study. The ultimate goal remains within view regardless of the level of operation.

Initiating the Independent Study Program

The key to the success of the independent study program is the faculty, who must believe in its benefits, desire to promote it, and work with students as individuals. Teachers who have consistently promoted student projects and other extra-class assignments are quick to recognize the merits of independent study. These teachers provide the foundation upon which to build, and they should be looked to for the leadership that is necessary if the program is to grow until it involves all of the students and faculty members. A school considering the organization of an independent study program should nurture these project-type activities and be alert for teachers who use them.

The method used to initiate independent study will vary from school to school, but a well-planned approach extended over a period of time is probably advisable. Such activities as in-service workshops, honor study halls, provision of study carrels for honor students, and school fairs featuring completed student projects will provide a good background for a successful program. The astute administrator will not suddenly announce in a faculty meeting: "Tomorrow, we will embark on a program of independent study." As the idea is developing, the staff, with the guidance of a materials' expert, should be adding books, supplies, and equipment so that when the big step is taken student initiative will not be frustrated by a lack of resources needed for the completion of a project. Physical arrangements must be prepared so that there will be a place for each student to work without supervision or interference. The traditional library or study hall will hamper independent work.

In spite of the careful preparations and the addition of facilities, problems will exist. One of the first is the re-education of both teachers and students. Teachers are slow to accept the idea that students can and should be allowed to organize their own work, plan their time, and work effectively without the presence of a teacher. Many teachers have a tendency to suspect any kind of schoolwork that cannot easily be classified as homework, and many students have been under close supervision so long that the withdrawal of supervision at first causes them to be uncomfortable and insecure. For example, a student studying the affairs of the world by reading *Time* magazine may be subject to suspicion, while one who studies his current events paper is obviously within his rights. The geometry teacher may take a dim view of a student who is reading a book on exploration of space instead of working his geometry problems. At Lakeview these difficulties arose in spite of the fact that every student assigned to a study carrel had a petition signed by all of his teachers stating that he was sufficiently self-directed to do all his studying independently. Since student homework assignments continued to come in on time and achievement increased, these doubts were largely eliminated.

Initially, the students, realizing that they had been given a position of trust through their assignment to an independent study carrel, resented interference by teachers; however, after a short time the relationship between students in carrels and teachers in team rooms became one of trust and confidence. The teachers learned that students could be trusted, and the students realized that teachers make excellent consultants in time of need.

A second problem is breaking from the tradition of the school's providing all of the do's and don't's necessary to control every situation. The students with study carrels had been given free access to any part of the instructional materials center with only this list of procedures to limit their activities:

1. No student is to leave the Instructional Materials Center except during the passing period.
2. Students are only permitted to have conferences upon the permission of a staff member, and these conferences are to take place only in one of the conference rooms.
3. Students are expected to work in a quiet, consistent fashion in the Instructional Materials Center.
4. Any students assigned to independent study who desire to leave the Instructional Materials Center or who desire not to go during the designated time must have informed the staff member in charge *before* the module.
5. The condition of the carrel is a personal responsibility of each student assigned to use it.

Pressure for specific rules by both teachers and students has been resisted; however, certain more definitive ground rules are under consideration.

After six months' experience with the Lakeview independent study program, there were still some faculty members who had never promoted the program with their students. They gave as the reason that if a student cannot complete his homework consistently, he certainly has no time for independent study. Because of this argument, the inclusion of homework in the study program was necessary. It was pointed out that those who are doing homework are working at the third level, and, without a revolutionary change in course goals or teacher activity, they could gradually advance to the higher levels. At first teachers seemed to envision a wide gap between the three levels of study. As this concept of continuous growth from one level to another became accepted, teachers began to allow and later to encourage student-assumed tasks to grow from their assigned work.

A criticism of the independent study program that is frequently expressed by visitors has proved to be unfounded after a year of operation. The criticism is an outgrowth of the fear that if it isn't known exactly what seat each student is using at a given time, the school is asking for trouble. To date, however, permanent seating has been unnecessary. The only complaint has been from counselors who have found that their counselees are more difficult to locate than they were when assigned to the traditional study hall. The granting of freedom within the confinement of the large instructional materials center has been enough of a security measure. It should be remembered that only students who have proved themselves to be self-directive are assigned there and they realize that one infraction causes loss of the privilege. Fewer problems exist with this situation than are typical with the library pass system used with the traditional study hall. The modular schedule eliminates much of the hall traffic because there is seldom a need for a teacher to issue corridor passes.

Most of the problems, both anticipated and actual, have eliminated themselves due to the fact that students basically want to learn. When given freedom to pursue knowledge without being inhibited by unnecessary rules and safeguards, they are careful not to abuse their privileges.

Team Teaching and Independent Study

A program of independent study can be successful in any school regardless of its organization, but its greatest promise is achieved in conjunction with team teaching. The arrangement of classes, the physical facilities, the cooperative tone, and the emphasis placed on the sharing of ideas in a school utilizing team teaching all have a stimulating effect on the effort of students to study independently. Teachers who are reluctant to attempt new ideas find themselves washed with the tide when they are placed on a team with people who are anxious to get things done. Soon they, too, become contributors to the common effort. If team meetings had no other advantages, they would be well worth the time and effort spent simply because they bring together regularly two or more people for the purpose of pooling their knowledge and talents in a cooperative teaching effort. Independent study flourishes under these conditions.

Sound educational thoughts, new ideas, and successful teaching techniques make the difference between mere mediocrity and true effectiveness in teaching. In the traditional classroom situation new innovations are often born with one teacher, used by him, and set aside until the following year when he teaches the same unit to a new group of students. There are too few opportunities for the transmission of skills from teacher to teacher, whereas team teaching allows for a pooling of the best techniques and thus new ideas are used not by one teacher but by many. If a thought occurs to a member of a teaching team, whether it concerns independent study, large-group presentations, or small-group techniques, it immediately becomes the property of the group. Their suggestions aid in the perfection of the idea, and it becomes a part of the teaching skill that benefits every student taking the course. These are some of the reasons that schools employing team teaching have quickly capitalized on its compatibility with independent study. It is a difficult job for a teacher working alone to continue to create ideas that will suggest independent study projects and stimulate the desire to learn for the sake of learning. Four good teachers who work together can maintain the interest and enthusiasm necessary to keep the students' incentive alive while these same teachers, working separately, may one or all have failed.

An example used by one team to sell independent study to its students is this bulletin prepared by the world history team and given to the students:

> We feel that up to this time we have only partially utilized the potential that the independent study portion of world history has to offer. The time that has been allotted to you (the student) for independent study, we hope you are using in a profitable manner. However, we feel that our expectations should be clarified so that complete understanding between student and teacher can exist.
>
> Although many students are not specifically assigned to study carrels in the IMC, time is nevertheless given to all students because

of the time structure of large and small group student contact. The remaining time SHOULD be used for the following types of student activities, which for all practical purposes can be called independent study:

a. *Additional Reading* from sources outside the text. This particular material may be teacher assigned or student assumed, but definitely should be aimed at bettering student insights in reference to the material under study.

b. *Individual Student-Teacher Conference.* We definitely want to encourage any and all students to feel absolutely free to consult with any instructor on the teaching team whenever a problem of interpretation, definition or understanding is encountered. Remember, (believe it or not) our job is to help students whenever we possibly can, but we must have your cooperation in enlisting and utilizing this potential aid.

c. *Individual Project Work.* This might be student assumed or teacher assigned, but we want this to be a valuable activity aimed at increasing your understanding of a problem or conflict that is truly recognized by student and/or teacher.

There is yet another dimension of independent study which has not been completely utilized nor understood. We speak now of a problem, project or other type of study which can exist beyond the basic curriculum and rises from the students' interests, desires, vocational or intellectual goals.

We would like to encourage any student who has a strong desire to extend his educational horizons beyond that set curriculum and into areas of profitable (and necessary) independent investigation to contact his small group teacher for further information and discussion of this area. (College bound students should definitely explore the possibilities that this program might offer them.)

The Flexible Schedule and Independent Study

In recent years more and more educators have questioned the assumption that all learning experiences should take place in the following environment:

1. A rectangular room must be provided. Best results will be obtained if there are enough cubic feet of space to provide air for forty or more people.

2. Chairs must be provided in neat rows and columns. At least thirty should be occupied by students of approximately the same age.

3. There must be a person in charge who is equally capable in handling all phases of the teaching process.

4. This environment must be provided at the same hour every day five days a week. There is often a further and well-advised stipulation that each hour should be broken someplace near the middle so that the students may prepare the next day's assignment.

5. This sequence is repeated for thirty-six to forty weeks. At the end of this time each student has presumably been exposed to the same amount of learning and is ready to be judged by measuring the amount that he has absorbed and retained.

Good teachers control the environment and do a good job. Poor teachers are controlled by the environment and seldom have the initiative or opportunity for growth.

The staff at Lakeview Junior-Senior High School is among those who have taken exception to these assumptions. Recognizing the unique nature of each of the many learning experiences in the secondary school curriculum, they have developed a schedule designed to provide the time, the space, the physical arrangement, and the class size most suitable for each learning group. This is the flexible schedule. It features three distinct types of learning activity: large-group instruction, small-group instruction and independent study.

Each year the individual departments decide what learning experiences will be provided in each of their courses, how often they will meet, how long each meeting shall be, and the recommended class size for each meeting. The administration then goes about the arduous task of constructing a schedule that will meet these needs. Chemistry, for example, meets in large groups for thirty minutes on Monday, Wednesday, and Friday and in small groups on Tuesday and Thursday for a period of ninety minutes. Additional time is provided in the laboratory for each student to engage in independent study. All students enrolled in chemistry are assigned to the large group and the small groups are limited to fifteen or less. General Mathematics meets on Tuesday and Thursday for a thirty-minute lecture followed immediately by a thirty-minute medium-sized class for supervised study and the opportunity for each member of the team to have a daily check on the progress of his students. They consider the daily collection of papers necessary for the slower students while in the higher mathematics courses independent study replaces the period following the lecture. On Mondays, Wednesdays, and Fridays, the general mathematics classes meet in small groups. Skill classes such as sewing, art, and woodworking generally meet for longer periods of time when they meet but meet less often.

In most cases the flexible schedule replaces two or three of the daily hour-long meetings with a half-hour lecture leaving both teachers and students time for involvement in the independent study program. Instead of the teacher spending his out-of-class time in the classroom, he returns to his desk in the instructional materials center where he is available to consult with students who are working in their study carrels. In order for the independent study program to be successful students must know when and where to go for teacher assistance.

Student time is scheduled in blocks when possible to allow some degree of completion once a task is begun. This is a typical student schedule:

HR.	M	T	W	T	F	COURSE	TEACHER	RM.
7	x		x			Independent Study		IMC
	x		x		x	World History	Bruce	127
8	x	x	x	x	x	Independent Study		IMC
9	x	x	x	x	x	Typing	Smith	212
10	x		x		x	Typing	Smith	212
	x		x			Independent Study - Typing		212
11				x		Health Class Activities		131
	x					Driver Ed.	Meyer	131
		x		x		English	Nelson	201
12	x	x	x	x	x	English	Nelson	201
13	x		x		x	English	Bangiolo	131
	x		x			Independent Study		IMC
14	x	x	x	x	x	Independent Study		IMC
15		x		x		Home Ec.	Abbott	114
	x		x		x	Independent Study		IMC

HR.	M	T	W	T	F	COURSE	TEACHER	RM.
1	x	x			x	Home Ec.	Abbott	112
		x		x		Independent Study		IMC
2	x	x			x	Home Ec.	Abbott	112
		x		x		Independent Study		IMC
3		x				Driver Ed.	Meyer	127
					x	Teentones	Placek	WH
			x	x		Independent Study-Home Ec.		112
4		x	x			Physical Educ. Dick		Gym
	x				x	Teentones	Placek	WH
			x			Independent Study		IMC
5		x		x		Physical Educ. Dick		Gym
	x	x			x	World History	Paulson	131
6		x	x		x	World History	Bruce	127
		x		x		Independent Study		IMC

Do you have brothers or sisters in LHS? Counselor:
Yes X   No   Older   Younger X
Homeroom 127

With the time provided, the director of the instructional materials center at hand, teacher assistance nearby, and all the books and equipment of the school at his disposal there is no limit to how far a student who wants to learn can go in his quest for knowledge.

The Student and Independent Study

When the Lakeview program was inaugurated, it was estimated that approximately seventy percent of the student body would profit from independent study. At present fifty-five percent are assigned permanently to study carrels and the other forty-five percent may go to the instructional materials center with passes signed by subject teachers. Experience has shown that not all students are sufficiently self-directed to operate in this new environment and not all students want to give up the security of the old-fashioned study hall. One of the top seniors last year refused the opportunity.

Selection of students is not on an ability basis. It has been found that some of the students from lower achievement levels make the best use of their study carrels. The quality of their work may be lower than the accelerated students, but their efforts are just as great and their behavior sometimes better. A greater percentage of the more gifted students become assigned to independent study because their minds seem to be challenged most through independent study. Intellectually able or not, the student who recognizes his goals and is willing to seek them usually wants and is given the opportunity to engage in independent study.

Student-assumed independent study projects begin with a proposal presented to the small-group teacher. It includes information about the nature of the project, the student's purpose, the resource material to be used, consultants, the type of evaluation and the end result. The following form is used for the proposal in one department:

LAKEVIEW INDEPENDENT STUDY   PROJECT NO._____

Name_____   Date_____

   I. Description of desired subject:

  II. Purpose(s) for entering into the project:

 III. Desired results and goals (list may be added to at any time):

 IV. Resources needed (list may be added to at any time):

  V. Desired type of evaluation:

       _____a. objective exam

       _____b. seminar with evaluative personnel

———————c. essay exam

———————d. oral exam administered by an evaluative committee made up of resource people

———————e. advanced placement exam

VI. Proposed length of project: (This would include comments which would relate to:)

a. when you intend to work on project

b. if this would include work over summer

c. project completion date

VII. Evaluation results:

The variety of projects is as wide as the interests of eleven hundred students, and resource materials and personnel are not limited to the school. A number of colleges have made their personnel and facilities available. One student's interest in international relations has resulted in a university's offer to provide visitors from foreign countries without cost to Lakeview's world history classes. Another student who wants to become a doctor prompted his teacher to get resource people from the medical profession. Local industries are interested in the program and are happy to assist. Every effort is made to provide the resources needed for any worthwhile independent study project.

Some student reactions are:

Bill Wolfe (Sophomore)

I am studying the life and writings of Ernest Hemingway at present. I have completed a number of projects this year including an analysis of "Ulalume" in English and a study of France from 1896 to 1919 in history.

The independent study program has broadened and stimulated my reading. The length of some of the topics has made conciseness and the ability to grab the fundamentals very important. I think it has helped my self-discipline to a certain extent.

William Fuller (Senior)

I am building a cloud chamber in physics and have completed a written project on the science of high explosives. I have developed a number of explosives in my laboratory at home.

The independent study program is O.K. It's the best way to get added knowledge on a subject.

Adrienne Reynolds (Sophomore)

I am working on a project in world history which will take me into the realm of ancient man and his movements. This will also deal with the formation of civilization and various geological aspects. (I plan to go into this field of study in college.)

In English, I have a tentative plan for a project on World War I and what it was like. This will include personal "eyewitness" reports from my grandfather who was in almost all of the major campaigns in France. I have completed a project in English on the origins of various expressions which came about because of personality quirks of certain people and why.

I think that the independent study program has basically a good beginning in our school. I think that it should include everyone regardless of ability because the students learn to complete a job independently. I think the program should include visits to research institutes that have an area of reference in the particular subject one has chosen. It might also include work over the summer for the students who are really interested in the subjects they have chosen. For instance, suppose a student is interested in archaeology, perhaps there would be someone interested enough in him to have a summer "job" on a "dig" to gain experience and to find out if he is really interested in that type of work.

George Taylor (Freshman)

I am not working on a project at present, but I have completed one in group guidance, one in English on mythology and one in science on biographies of famous men in electronics.

I think the independent study program is tremendous.

Bonnie Baker (Sophomore)

The Life and Works of Walt Whitman is my eighth project this year. Others include: The Political Parties of France, the Economy of France, the Mysteries of Psychology, America's Racial Problem, the Evils of Daydreaming, the Life and Works of Washington Irving, and a special report on Gunnar Myrdal's "An American Dilemma."

In my opinion the independent study program is the ideal way to educate young people. It gives the individual student the opportunity to do research at any time. There is always help available from the teachers.

Danny Potts (Sophomore)

I am working on five independent study projects at the present time. None of these is required. They are: The "Isms", Past and Present; Radioactive Dating of Mica; Solid Geometry for Proficiency Examination; Point Number—Line Number Correlation; and Russian Culture Studies. In the past year I have completed these projects: *Plato's Republic; Julius Caesar;* and I completed the Algebra 3 course by using programmed learning materials and a proficiency test.

Independent study is a step away from the traditional and a step nearer the goal—critical thinking with facts as the building materials rather than as the tools.

Paulette Scales (Junior)

I believe the independent study program is very worthwhile and that it fits very well with the Decatur-Lakeview Plan. It gives the student the opportunity to be more or less on his own and to have the responsibility of doing his own work and taking care of the equipment available to him. Although some students don't take advantage of this, the majority do.

Sue Burns (Senior)

I am doing research on that part of physics which applies to nursing. I plan to enter nurse's training next fall.

Facilities for Independent Study

As mentioned earlier, good results can be obtained in any school regardless of organization or facilities, but a well-equipped instructional materials center with carrels to provide individual privacy for the students and adjacent team rooms for the teachers offers the ideal situation. The IMC is the center of most of the learning activities at Lakeview. A well-stocked and capably staffed IMC is a solid foundation for any independent study program.[2]

The instructional materials center at Lakeview has been designed to bring teachers, students, and materials together. An attempt has been made to provide a completely self-contained center with everything needed to allow students to engage in independent study with no need for interruption.

The Role of the Teacher

The teacher is the key to the success of the independent study program. His own desire for knowledge, his interest in students, and his leadership are reflected in the work of his students. He must replace the artificial incentives of grades and awards with the only true incentive —a thirst for knowledge. The teacher who does the best job of selling independent study to his students is one who believes that the ultimate outcome of education is the development of people who:

1. have a wide breadth of interests and experiences
2. possess the ability to locate needed information
3. have highly developed skills of communication
4. have some special talents or fields of specialization

Some teacher comments are:

Mr. Robert Flaugher (Boys' Physical Education)

Independent study develops within the students the ability and desire to keep on learning after the completion of their formal schooling. I don't believe it has even begun to grow to its potential; however, strides are being made in that direction. One thing to consider would be extending the hours of the IMC beyond the school day.

Mr. David Rayhill (Industrial Arts)

I think the concept is ideal, and implementing it in the industrial arts area is not difficult. We have boys working on programmed learning texts in electronics, and most of those enrolled in regular courses are working on individual projects in the shop.

Miss Virginia Casey (English)

Independent study is a necessary part of the Decatur-Lakeview Plan. Coverage of the year's materials and development cannot be accomplished in the large and small groups alone. Independent study permits the full program to operate.

Adequate and pertinent research material is vital to the proper functioning of the IMC. Here the student can find facts, motivation and enrichment for creativity and for thoughtful analysis of many topics.

The program is continually improving as students master knowledge of subject, location of material, and technique of research reporting. The English teaching teams are in the process of revising the "total instructional package" for 3-way learning: large group, small group and independent study.

Mr. Dan Andersen (Social Studies)

Teacher assignments for independent study should be made according to the ability of the student. Some students must utilize every minute to keep up with the regular assignments while others need worthwhile projects and activities to make school more meaningful. In order to encourage independent study and to make the work of the students most effective every teacher should work meetings in the IMC into his lesson plans on a regular basis.

Mr. L. K. Philbrook (Physics and Chemistry)

The idea of independent study is good for the gifted student. The student selects the subject he wants to work on. It can be of a research nature followed by laboratory work or strictly exploratory in nature. The teacher serves chiefly as a resource person but often as an instigator to ideas.

Miss Marilyn Dongowski (English)

Students in the upper half of their classes profit most from independent study. Lower ability students tend to copy material rather than assimilate it. Perhaps, too many projects are required on time for a grade, and this "assignment" then nips in the bud some more scholarly pursuit.

Students are using the instructional materials center much more than students ordinarily use a library. I see more and more student-initiated use of facilities. Some students are developing an intellectual curiosity. Many students feel that required projects are stultifying.

When the urge to do independent study is as "catching" as the flu "bug," we will have arrived.

Mrs. Marilyn Fleener (Home Economics)

The concept of independent study is good, generally—particularly, excellent in home economics. Students should not be pushed into independent study in all areas.

Miss Arline Stokes (English)

Independent study is an excellent plan by which students can explore and develop topics of genuine interest to them. Because the student is stimulated toward the completion of self-determined goals, the results of independent study surpass in many cases the student's previous achievement level. Through independent study, flexibility of curriculum and allowances for individual differences enter the school program.

The Future of Independent Study

After a year of operation at Lakeview the independent study program is still in its infancy, but it is growing rapidly. At this early stage of development there have been no opportunities for students to take courses for credit that are not offered in the regular curriculum. This is one of the greatest promises of independent study and there are two plans underway that should be ready by 1965-66.

The first of these plans is the development of an independent physical education program. This program will be conducted in a separate room under the gymnasium bleachers which will be called the "Body Building Lab." The scope of the program will include the development of independent study projects by students in the areas of (1) prescribed exercise for many of those presently excused for medical reasons, (2) body building, including muscular, cardiovascular, and coordinative development for the atypical student and (3) a general physical fitness program for the normal. These activities will be interspersed with team play and carry-over activities. Vigorous activity will be stressed in most of the activities, and library research will be required of each student.

The other program presently under consideration will offer students the opportunity to complete present courses in less time and work in areas of their choice for the remainder of the year. They will also be able to follow courses of study not included in the present curriculum and receive high school credit upon completion. Each student when admitted to the program will be given a course of study geared to that particular subject field. This will include basic text readings and supplementary reading with a representative of the appropriate teaching team assigned as consultant and advisor. The student will be expected to utilize this person whenever the need arises. In addition to the readings the course of study will include tapes of lectures, filmstrips, films, seminars, conferences with the IMC director and outside resource people, and programmed learning units. After a study of student and teacher interests a summer workshop will be set up to allow teachers to plan the courses of study. Two courses being planned at this time are Economics and International Relations.

The independent study program requires hard work, ingenuity, careful planning, and the desire to work with students in a personal relationship. The school that tries it will find its efforts well-rewarded with the increased educational opportunities offered its students.

CHAPTER 5

Practices and Programs for Elementary Schools

by

ANNE PATRICK

Anne Patrick has been an instructor at the University School, Indiana University, for three years. Before joining the staff in Bloomington she taught in the elementary schools in Mentor, Ohio. Her master's degree is from Indiana University.

EDUCATORS in elementary schools are exploring exciting new programs which nurture independent study as a frequently used mode of instruction. New and better ways of educating the nation's children are being developed by creative teachers and administrators who are swept up in a feeling of nearly evangelistic urgency to improve the quality of elementary school education. Once cautiously avoided in the public schools, innovation has become a common and valued practice.

Independent study is a foundation of some of the most significant educational innovations which have gathered momentum recently. With its emphasis upon varying the size of instructional groups (large group, small group, and independent study), the Trump Plan has had impact on encouraging the use of independent study in the high school. Stimulated by the development of experimental programs such as those at Harvard (the SUPRAD Program) and Claremont Graduate School in California, the team teaching movement awakened interest in independent study for the elementary school. The movement toward nongraded schools and programs of continuous education has focused attention upon the individual learner. Rapid development of educational technology, especially programmed learning, closely relates to the growing interest in independent study.

Dr. Robert Anderson,[1] provocative Harvard University educator, recently pointed to team teaching, nongraded schools, and independent study as three innovations which hold great promise for the improvement of American education in the immediate future. A dynamic relationship exists between team teaching, the nongraded school, and independent study. However, to understand the interrelatedness of these concepts, it is helpful to examine them separately. Then, they can be ordered in a system of instruction. Team teaching centers around the activities of the teaching staff; the nongraded school concept is organized around content mastery and skill development primarily; the independent study notion is concerned basically with a method for children's procedures and involvement in the learning process.

The trend toward the use of independent study as a mode of learning grows out of an increasing concern for the particular educational development of each individual. Independent study programs are a practical way to compensate for individual differences among elementary school youngsters. Early attempts to deal with individual differences focused primarily on varying instruction for groups of students, as illustrated by concern for homogeneous groups, achievement groups, interest groups, track plans, and so forth. Grouping emphasis of the elementary school centered typically on reading groups and committee work in science and social studies. However, the individual has not been entirely overlooked as evidenced by the Pueblo Plan, Dalton Plan, and Winnetka Plan.[2]

Since the renewed focus on independent study owes much to its intimate association with the Trump Plan,[3] independent study is often mentioned with large- and small-group instruction. In the Trump Plan the implementation of the three concepts—independent study, large- and small-group instruction—has found most of its application at the secondary school level. There has been little independent study at the elementary level, but it usually has been within the structure of the self-contained classroom and as an adjunct to group instruction. However, it finds its fullest potential in the nongraded school organized around teaching teams.

Independent Study Defined

As a method of teaching, independent study develops in the child, with careful and special assistance from the teacher, responsibility and freedom to think and study on his own in one or more areas of interest for a varying period of time, depending on the defined task. Many times he may be free to choose and describe his own learning objectives, as well as to select methods to obtain them. The student will personally devise his own means of reporting and evaluating his achievement. This type of study not only aims at the intellectually able but also provides these opportunities for all students, assuming that a high degree of self-education will take place in the process.

The concept of independent study is not totally new. One can recall seat work, homework, special projects, study halls, honors work, contract plans, and other related procedures. However, the concept has been refined with more emphasis on independent study replacing group teaching methods.

Three Levels

Three levels of independent study should be identified and described. The first, seatwork or guided study, involves independent effort. As a type of independent study, it calls for teacher direction and represents a closed-end activity. For example, fifty arithmetic problems are assigned to all students. After each student completes the assignment, he is finished. Little relationship is established between any one task and the succeeding task. In the past much seat work, composed mostly of drill or practice type activities, was given to individual students in order to maintain order in the classroom. Little attention was given to individual learning objectives.

The second level of individual study also represents a teacher-directed situation. However, the assignment is left open-ended, and no limit is placed on what the student may do. For example:

1. See how many different ways you can solve the following problem—236
   48
   +375

(The possibilities are infinite if you really *understand* basic mathematical principles.)

2. Write a story suggested by these three words: ball, bat and trouble.
3. How many new words can you spell if you know how to spell "same"? (fame, game, blame, shame, etc.)

These kinds of learning assignments help youngsters gather information and teach them to use it in both an orderly and a creative way. Students are not harnessed to single-answer responses. They are given the opportunity to work at their own rate and level of ability.

The highest level of individual study provides for individual pursuit. The student assumes responsibility for identifying his problem, topic, or area of study. The student's area of investigation comes from a school's course or study guide and from the student's experiential background. In elementary school a close relation to the stated curriculum usually exists, particularly where teacher-pupil planning is stressed. Teachers should introduce the skills or content to be taught, and children should select the means by which this content is to be studied and used. The possibilities for individual variation in learning assignments are limitless. Some of the concerns or study areas identified by children will not relate to a basic curriculum guide developed by teachers. The guide becomes the student's interest, not the printed page of the curriculum outline. If the pupils are encouraged to explore their own ideas even though not in the curriculum *per se*, they are operating on a high level of independent study. Once the problem or area of investigation has been identified, the teacher shifts the focus to available resources and means of securing ideas and information. Students are encouraged to read widely, think critically, develop generalizations, and form opinions.

Occasionally a child will branch off into some phase of study which has not had its motivational roots in the classroom. However, it takes time and experience for a child to develop a high degree of independence from teacher suggestions in carrying through independent study interests. Elementary school teachers will have to do more suggesting of topics in the early years of schooling than will teachers in the later years. Teachers must determine instructional objectives, arouse interest, suggest methods of study, and consult with children as they carry on their own work. Before an independent study activity exists, the youngster has to accept the objective (perhaps without realizing it), become interested in the topic, use a variety of resources, and give serious thought to the problem. The approaches used in studying a topic will range from student to student, depending on the interest and ability of the child. The depth and breadth of investigation is to be correlated with the ability of the child. Each independent study project must be evaluated in the shadow of the child's unique abilities, rather than against group norms.

Goals and Objectives

As knowledge of how children learn is accumulated, the teacher will want to reevaluate the way she teaches. Elementary school teachers must spend considerable time and effort keeping abreast of the new curricula and the emerging theories of teaching. The last college course in educational methodology can only be thought of as a background for a continuing study of professional techniques of teaching. It has been said that this is the age of an instructional revolution. New curricula and substantially different teaching methods are the manifestations of the revolution in elementary school education.

Since education is a never-ending process continuing into adulthood it necessitates the development of personal responsibility and positive attitudes toward learning. This means learning must be personally pleasing and backed up with individual success. Humans are prone to continue to do those things they are good at doing; they engage in activities from which they get personal satisfaction. If a solid interest in learning is to be a lifetime pursuit, it needs to be a thrilling and profitable enterprise for each child in the elementary school. Success builds on success. Regardless of scholastic capacity, all youngsters can achieve success on their level of understanding. It is the demanding task of the teacher to structure learning experiences appropriate to the abilities of each learner. This means that independent study activities will vary significantly from child to child. Some children, of course, will be able to be successful on higher levels than others and in different areas.

The goal of independent study is to bring a child to the thrilling realization that he can learn something almost anytime and nearly anywhere. To instill in the youngster the inordinate desire to learn on his own, bounded by nothing but his own resources and ambitions, is the abiding mission of the elementary school teacher. The more personalized instruction becomes, the greater will be its immediate impact and enduring value.

The major objective of independent study is to bring the individual to a mastery of himself. Secondary goals of independent study are to:

1. Help the student learn to study
2. Provide an opportunity for creative thinking and exploration
3. Encourage analytical and critical thinking through emphasis on inquiry
4. Provide an opportunity for the student's pursuit of individual interests
5. Overlap an interest in learning through successful intellectual effectiveness

The process of inquiry is far more important than the specific information assimilated. Knowing facts and handling fundamental processes are rudimentary. Real education begins when children use the facts they know and the processes they command. Independent study helps youngsters take the big step from knowing to understanding and using ideas and processes. This means that the elementary school classroom is a laboratory for individual work more than a cell for teacher-dominated exercises.

The sign of a good school is one in which the children feel a strong responsibility for what goes on in their school-community and in their classroom. They are involved. They make decisions about their learning and they carry on their own work. Attitudes of later life are developed during the elementary school years. Therefore, independent thought and responsibility should be stressed in first years of schooling. The way youngsters begin their school careers will have a profound influence on the successive stages of those careers. Independent study should begin with the first year of schooling. One does not suddenly reach the age of twenty-one and become an independent, responsible individual. Dependence is a learned trait. So is independence. Educating for individual responsibility and personal achievement is not an easy task, but must be the concern of all elementary school teachers.

An old Chinese proverb says, "Study without thought is useless, thought without study is dangerous." Thought and study are vital to the effective individual study program. Young children need opportunities for practice and drill. These activities are essential to the mastery of basic skills. The notion that independent study is to be reserved for enrichment activities is fallacious. Students can do much of the needed drill and practice as part of their independent study work. However, the requirements for this type of activity vary markedly from child to child. Even at early stages of formal education opportunities for individualized learning should be provided. As teachers meet with youngsters in conferences professional judgments can be made about the kind and sphere of independent study a child should engage in.

Society is begging for men with original ideas in all areas of inquiry and for leaders who can make rapid intellectual advancements with a creative substance that looks upon change as a challenge. As a teacher works with a child, every possible attempt should be made to stretch the youngster's imagination, spark his creative tendencies, and feed an interest in discovery.

The preparation of boys and girls for vibrant lives which contribute to society is not easy to describe with precision. The society for which today's youngsters are being prepared is, after all, unknown and uncharted. It is possible, and the only sensible alternative, to develop traits of responsibility and independence of thought. Unless a school has a planned program for nurturing independence and instilling responsibility for learning, prospects of enlarging these traits are not likely to be positive.

Description of Independent Study Activities

In the preceding discussion the focus has been on the general educational scene in which independent study may evolve and upon the definition and goals of such a program. It may be helpful to turn attention to some actual descriptions of independent study activities for the elementary school.[4]

The seven descriptions that follow represent a mere sampling of the myriad of possibilities for developing independent study activities in the elementary school. They are offered as suggestions and illustrations for discussion rather than to provide ideal models. The purpose is to open the door in the hope that others will be encouraged to take these or other steps in developing independent study programs.

Example One:

Following an earthquake crisis in Alaska, students chose study topics from an earlier investigation of Alaska. Each explored to varying depths the crisis and its far-reaching effects, not only on Alaska but the other states and the world. The effects on Alaska's development in political, social, economic, cultural, educational, and physical areas of thought were discussed generally by class groups.

Individual students selected special areas of interest to study in depth. These studies allowed each student to explore a particular interest and to develop a greater understanding of some aspect of this project. The studies were carried on within the regular school day with the teacher at hand to give individual assistance to each student as the need arose. Trips to the school library, consultation with a person who had been to Alaska, and the viewing of a filmstrip were the part of different students' data-gathering procedures.

Reports were written, largely done at home. Trips to the dictionary and to reference sources were required. These reports contained a statement of the purpose of the particular study and gave the sources from which the students got their information. Class presentations were made by each investigator with questions asked by the other members of the class.

Students evaluated their own work, and the teacher pointed out both strengths and weaknesses to the students in private follow-up conferences.

Example Two:

A room library was developed by a group of interested students for independent study and class reading purposes. Objects that could be borrowed from home to add to its attractiveness and function were brought in by the students. The children alternated responsibility for operating the library facilities and taking care of the reference and pleasure reading materials. A strong feeling of pride and accomplishment, first exhibited by few, soon spread throughout the class and even to the community. People who heard about the class activity sent gift books and other materials, such as sets of *National Geographic* magazines.

Individual students made visual displays to encourage others to read a greater variety of books. A Ten Keys Club was formed in the class. Each key represented a different category of reading and every child, as he finished a book, recorded it on a chart and reviewed the book with another student. This laid the basis for annotated book lists developed by the class. Certain bibliographic information and brief descriptions of the book or magazine were given. Evaluations of the books were made by the students. The range of reading and the quality of reports were fantastically wide.

Example Three:

A science area in one classroom provided a place for spontaneous collections, such as fossils brought in from an afternoon recess. Microscopic studies of insects, algae, and other specimens were made. Individual experiments were displayed in the science area. It goes without saying that order took a back seat to the disarray which resulted from the work of scientific discovery in this center. The children learned about the proper care of instruments and materials, but housekeeping was of secondary importance to the activities.

Each child kept a science notebook which he designed and organized. One interesting section of the notebook was the "thought page," where the children jotted down original ideas, questions, and topics for future research.

Research of a high quality was carried on by these youngsters at their level of understanding. While their conclusions were not new to the field of science, they were searching inquiries for the children and gave fresh ideas to the young researchers. Students not only studied about science and scientists, but they were scientists themselves.

Example Four:

A class "literature book," to which any child could make a contribution in creative writing was a vehicle used for individual expression in one room. Unusual objects and illustrations of many varied types were displayed about the room. These often served as stimulators to ideas which triggered students' creative written expression. Many of the stories eventually found their way into the school and community newspapers.

No child was required to write but all had the opportunity to do so. When a paper was completed, it was read to a small group or to the entire class. Both the content and mechanics of composition were discussed. Most children liked to write and sensed a thrill at seeing their work in the class literature book. Some of the able students wrote many stories, others fewer. The amount of effort, the teacher felt, was as great for the voluminous authors as for those who struggled with fewer stories. Some stories were long and involved. Others were short and crisp. The quality varied.

Each child was given assistance in spelling the words he wanted to use in the sentences. The teacher encouraged the children in individual conferences to go to various sources for ideas and for new words. Vocabulary was increased, the teacher felt, by using new words in sentences, rather than by memorizing them in lists. Once children had this kind of experience and sense of accomplishment, it was relatively easy to introduce means by which their writing could be improved.

Example Five:

One teacher set aside a block of time each morning for independent reading or free study. During this time students selected a problem and then worked at whatever phase of it they wanted to investigate. Instead of typical seat work, students did creative writing, worked with various types of art media, researched some phase of the social studies, experimented in science, and spent time on investigations of their choosing. Creative writing took many forms, from poems to short stories to full-length books. Since many children were talented in music, this time was also used to author original songs, interpret music, and make variations of musical selections. A tape recorder was used to capture their creative attempts to combine certain sounds of musical instruments. Often the art work one child did was related to the work of others. Some illustrated stories; others made maps or pictures for use with a social studies project.

Example Six:

Many attempts at independent study grew out of the unit approach to teaching in the various subject-matter areas. In a study of sea animals, two pupils volunteered to research a particular animal of interest. The product of the students' work took the form of a written and an oral report. Also, they made a descriptive chart. The information gathered was usually factual including descriptive data, habitats, food, habits, and so forth.

Other independent study projects were less factual and formal in approach, yet they involved depth study. For example, in a social studies unit on pioneers, each pupil was asked to identify as many ways as possible to travel across the country, necessities needed for the trip, and dangers that might be encountered. Furthermore, they were required to justify their contentions. More frequently resources were used, and each child developed his own set of plans regarding the trip across country.

Example Seven:

A series of "morning talks" was introduced. Every day students were asked to prepare a four-minute presentation. The class was divided into small groups so that every student would be able to present his ideas and all students had the opportunity to increase their listening and questioning skills. The subject of the talk was sometimes determined by the student and sometimes selected by the group itself. Most frequently the talk was an outgrowth of a special pupil investigation.

Once a week a list was posted in the room and pupils signed up for a certain date and topic and listed the length of time needed for a major presentation for all the class. These were voluntary presentations. Many pupils preferred this method of sharing their knowledge to that of writing or engaging in art or scientific work.

Other Programs

As interest in independent study increases, more descriptive material will be found in the literature. Some interesting programs have already been developed. For example, in Winnetka, Illinois, the emphasis at Skokie Junior High School has been on the development of Learning Laboratories.[5] Here students are given an opportunity for unstructured inquiry and the pursuit of intellectual studies important to each student as an individual. Self-instruction, self-motivation, and independent inquiry characterize the work carried on in the laboratory. The laboratory itself, which consists primarily of a room filled with the newer media of instruction, is being developed in harmony with the conventional library. Students are released from their regular classroom for various amounts of time in order to work on personal (or sometimes teacher-assigned) pursuits of independent study. The director of the learning laboratory works closely with classroom teachers and students.

That learning laboratories, such as the one described above, are also becoming increasingly important at the elementary school level is evidenced by the work currently underway in Shaker Heights, Ohio.[6] The focus in Shaker Heights has centered on the development of work-study skills and independent study habits for pupils in the fourth, fifth, and sixth grades.

To help learn self-directed independent study habits a learning center has been developed in two schools. In addition to a vast array of reading materials, each center is equipped with study carrels, each with an electrical outlet and a filmstrip viewer. Listening areas have also been established where students can plug in earphones and listen to tapes and records. Programmed materials are available in three areas: organizing and reporting; reading graphs, charts, and tables; and basic library skills.

The laboratory school at Brigham Young University, Provo, Utah, is implementing a new design for public school organization of the curriculum.[7] As with other new programs, the emphasis is upon the individual and his continuous educational progress. At the present time materials are being designed for independent study. Such development is currently in the embryonic stage but it will ultimately take the form of auto-instructional material. Spaces for individual, small-group, and large-group instruction are provided in Provo. Each pupil has a study carrel of his own, equipped with the latest technological intercommunication devices. Individualized approaches are being developed for the teaching of most subjects.

The Future

The instructional materials center will be the heart of many schools in the future. Project rooms and work areas make up a substantial part of the center, which also houses all of the printed and audiovisual resources a school can amass. Students will have easy and frequent access to the instructional materials center. Some areas will be set aside for noisy activities, others for work which requires quiet. The classroom will be an extension of the instructional materials center. A teacher, other than the classroom teacher, will be on hand to guide students and answer questions in the instructional materials center.

Eventually elementary students will spend a large amount of their time in school in independent study activities. Much of this work will be accomplished in carrels which are arranged centrally and adjacent to materials centers. The carrels and the center will be equipped with individual television screens; earphones and facilities for dialing for video-tape presentations and demonstrations; a signal device for notifying teachers as assistance is needed; monaural tape of lectures, speeches, foreign language lessons, and music; teaching machines; and a wide variety of reference books, periodicals, and other reading materials.

The school's physical facilities will change to accommodate the requirements of independent study in the elementary school. Existing space will be converted from group instructional areas to individual learning areas. This is discussed in more detail in Chapter Ten.

The Teacher

The final success of independent study will depend upon the person who actually puts it into effect, the classroom teacher. A teacher needs to be willing, even eager, to encourage independent study. This is the same kind of desire for personal satisfaction as the child who wants to find out why thunder booms or what makes a desert. The teacher who has a curious mind and sincerely enjoys new explorations will like to work with independent study. She will willingly forsake the single text and happily work with individuals more than with groups. The enthusiasm a teacher feels for independent study is transmitted to her students. The teacher who will be effective in nurturing independent study will not be one who wants her class neatly organized with each child rigidly attempting to cover the same material or one who looks upon any interruption of her planned activities or deviation from the curriculum guide as a minor irritation.

The teacher in a successful independent study operation must be ready to accept change, change in plans, in activities, in work habits, and in teaching procedures. She is no longer the source of all knowledge, the lecturer, the explainer, the assignment giver; rather, she is the counselor, the guide, the listener, and the friend of her students. She will help children steer away from unproductive activities, help them use resources properly, encourage them with the patience of Job. She must be the kind of person who is willing to give free rein to children to work outside her circle of influence and to respond to any accomplishment, even though she has not been at the center of the learning experience.

In the self-contained classroom it has been tempting to keep a tight rein on what every Johnny and Jane learns. When the child moves across those invisible boundaries of what has been planned in a curriculum guide or lesson plan book, the teacher may feel threatened and become uncomfortable. It is almost as if she could be thinking, "If I let Johnny learn on his own, pretty soon, if he finds enough good sources, he may know more than I do." This state of affairs should be the goal not the threat. When a teacher has the responsibility for as many as six or seven subjects, when time for extensive outside reading is limited and when she is dealing with sharp students, it is not unlikely that in some areas students may learn and deal with ideas foreign to the teacher. The only thing that could be wrong with this is that the teacher does not develop new knowledge and encourage the student in his pursuits. Students should be free to explore, question, and think.

Another important job of the teacher in independent work is to provide feedback to the children. Elementary children need to have their work recognized in one way or another. They want and have a right to the teacher's critical and positive evaluation of their efforts. This may be done in any number of ways, through discussion, by placing work on display, with written comments, in reports to the class, or through a note to the parents.

Pupils should work toward defined goals in their independent study program. These objectives should be understood by the student. Without clearly defined and broadly conceived objectives, the activity will not reach its full value for the long-range educational development of the child. Part of the thrill for any traveler is to know how far he is from his destination. Students want to know, and profit from knowing, how they are doing.

At the beginning of the school year, the teacher needs to work with her group in order to find out what kinds of experiences they have had in independent study. She needs to know what kind of environment will help children discover and develop areas which will be of interest to them. In summary her tasks boil down to five significant jobs:

1. To motivate the student toward whatever level of independent study appears most appropriate for him.
2. To counsel the student regarding his area of concern and guide him to the resources to enrich the area.
3. To teach him the effective use of multiple resources.
4. To continue to encourage and aid him as he works toward his goals.
5. To recognize his efforts and evaluate his products.

To those teachers who doubt the value of independent study in the elementary school, there can be only one comment: Try it for a sustained period of time and thrill to the advantages to you, and, more important, to your students!

CHAPTER 6

The Brookhurst Junior High School Program

by

Gardner A. Swenson

During the time Gardner A. Swenson has been principal of the Brookhurst Junior High School in Anaheim, California, the staff has developed a unique flexible scheduling program, which relies heavily on the use of independent study. Mr. Swenson is also an instructor at Chapman College in Orange, California. He is a graduate of the University of Utah and has served on the summer faculty of Brigham Young University in Provo, Utah.

AFTER A HALF CENTURY of development, the junior high program is still the center of controversy. Modern proponents of the junior high school appear to be no nearer solutions to the many educational problems than were the faculty members of the first junior high school of January, 1910, in Berkeley, California. In fact, the problems faced by today's junior high school educator appear more critical and insurmountable. Recently in a principal's meeting the junior high teachers of science and English petitioned for more time of the school day for instruction; the foreign language teachers requested additional time in order to implement the State of California law requiring foreign language for all pupils in the seventh and eighth grades, and the elective teachers protested the petitions of the academic teachers. Perhaps there is some justification for the protests as they are beginning to feel the squeeze for time and students.

Today's problems appear to center around competition by teachers for time rather than a concern for the improvement of quality in the junior high school educational program. The approach of compromising one subject for another continues to create one crisis after another for the junior high school. The controversy now raging in the junior high will decrease only when more attention is given to the learning theory in the instructional methods associated with the curriculum. Instead of participation in continuous arguments over the merits of the core versus departmentalization, the place of the ninth grade, what grade level science should be taught, and the requirements for junior high school graduation, the time would be better spent studying the growth and developmental characteristics of the junior high school age youngster and improving the quality of his educational program.

> The significance of the multisensory approach, of learning by doing, of generalization, of planned reinforcement, and of other facets of learning theory must be implemented into a quality instructional program.[1]

Although the junior high school teacher plans an educational program for the group, usually leveled for the average, he agrees that the greatest need of the young adolescent is help in achieving identity as an individual, both as a learner and as a citizen in a democratic society. The teacher is eager to teach critical thinking, to use the problem-solving approach, and to break the lockstep that marches the able student with the average and frustrates the remedial student with a fast pace. However, no matter how he tries to improve the quality of instruction for his students who come to him in groups of thirty-five, six times a day, he is defeated by the inherited characteristics of the junior high school organization and pattern—a structure that controls his time, his methodology, the size of his group, the number of his students, and his physical environment.

The structural weaknesses in the junior high school that prohibit individualization and a quality instructional program must be eliminated. A look at the history of education reveals previous attempts, as reported in Chapter Two.

> Supervised study and group study were introduced in order to get pupils to do more work for themselves. "Dalton" schools sprang up and "contracts" were popular with their minimum and maximum

assignments. There were also the Morrison techniques. All these were good because they moved teachers closer to the needs of the individual children.[2]

The solution to the problems of the junior high school must be found in the recognition and the acceptance of the needs and characteristics of the junior high school age pupil. Then a program must be systematically developed and executed to eliminate the present evils of a system that is organized on the following assumptions:

1. That all subjects in the junior high school should be given equal time regardless of the importance or value placed upon them by society, i.e., reading versus basket-weaving.
2. That all students are the same in ability, needs, and interests. The concept behind the time schedule of the traditional school is that every child needs exactly the same number of minutes of instruction in each subject as every other child, i.e., a pupil with third grade reading ability compared with a pupil reading at the tenth grade level.
3. That students grow uniformly; therefore, a new master schedule is not necessary because growth must be constant or fixed.
4. That administrators know best and should dole out time, number of students, facilities, and methodology to the teacher regardless of her professional training and ability.
5. That all teachers possess with equal efficiency and effectiveness those abilities necessary for a quality instructional program.
6. That the junior high school age youngster is not mature enough to make decisions regarding the use he will make of the time during the school day.

Junior high school administrators and classroom teachers constantly need to seek new ways of organizing classes, new methods of instruction, and new ways of utilizing staff resources so that a junior high school structure serving the needs of the preadolescent can be incorporated into the present system. Fortunately, there are innovating educators concerned with the need to improve the quality of the educational program in the junior high school.

The promise of a quality junior high school program is outlined in the findings and recommendations of the Commission on Experimental Study of the Utilization of the Staff in the Secondary School,

Focus on Change: Guide to Better Schools by Dr. J. Lloyd Trump, Director of the Commission, and Dorsey Baynham and *Images of the Future: A New Approach to the Secondary School* by Dr. Trump.

In an article entitled "Developing a More Dynamic Junior High School Program," Dr. Trump presents the following suggestions for a more dynamic junior high school program:

1. Develop more personal student responsibility for learning.
2. Use programmed instruction devices to permit different rates of progress by students.
3. Improve students' communication, problem solving, and critical thinking skills.
4. Develop better interpersonal relations among students.
5. Provide a curricular organization that furnishes essential content in all areas of human knowledge, keeps students continuously in contact with all the areas, stimulates student interests and talents, encourages creativity, and provides opportunities for studies in depth.

Objectives and Purposes of Independent Study in the Junior High School

Why eliminate the counselor's favorite dumping ground, the study period? Why ask the principal to give away his symbol of status and security, the master schedule? Why build a library larger than the gym as Dr. Frank Brown has done at Melbourne High School in Florida? Why take hours of teacher time to conduct in-service training workshops on methods used in large groups, small discussion groups, and independent study? These questions must be answered to the satisfaction of the junior high school teachers and administrators before changes take place. The rewards of independent study must be greater for the student before the educator spends energy and time developing a flexible schedule, building a functional plant, or conducting workshops to develop an effective faculty.

The answer to these questions must be found in the objectives of independent study in the junior high school.

1. The use of independent study permits different rates of progress by students. The range of student abilities becomes well-defined at

the junior high school level as evidenced by the chart showing a range of physical, intellectual, and aptitude factors of eighth grade students from Brookhurst Junior High School in Anaheim, California.

AGE:	13.9	to	15.9
HEIGHT:	4'11"	to	6'1"
WEIGHT:	85 lbs.	to	205 lbs.
I.Q.:	56	to	154
READING:	3.4	to	11.9

Pupil differences appear to be exaggerated at this level. The needs of the gifted students provide a challenge to the junior high school teachers. One method of meeting this challenge has been to let the student skip grades or in some other way to move on ahead of his peer group. Teachers have expressed concern regarding the time and material needed to meet the challenge of the gifted student. Independent study provides many different types of student activities: reading, observing, listening, writing, and automated learning devices. Students should have opportunities to reach in all directions for educational goals and experiences as dictated by their needs, abilities, and interests. As Dr. Trump expresses it, "The basic philosophy in recognizing individual differences among students is to provide a clinical approach to each student."[3]

2. The contract elective concept of independent study is an answer to the competition for time during the school day between the elective subject and academics. At the junior high school level all students should study each year all areas of knowledge, including the humanities, mathematics, science, practical and creative art, as well as health and physical education. Still important is the original purpose of the junior high school, to explore.

Pressures created by competition for time need not eliminate certain elective courses from the curriculum. There is a need to replace the present required and elective courses with a balance through the use of independent study and the "contract elective." A daily schedule including independent study is determined each day. The schedule is based upon the performance needs and potential of each pupil; consequently, students do not need to meet in each course each day for a specific period of time, but the time of the school day must be flexible enough to be controlled by the decisions of the pupil and teacher. Daily progress and movement of the pupil through the school day is determined by his readiness to accept the next goal or concept. Acceptance of new goals or even subjects need not be synonymous with years, quarters, or semesters. Independent study in the contract electives will preclude the possibility of a pupil being forced to drop violin because he needs a foreign language although the school day need not necessarily be lengthened.

3. The junior high school has a particular responsibility for helping pupils to learn how to study. A more independent approach to studying is required of them at this level. Even well-motivated students need to learn the techniques of studying. Large quantities of inappropriate homework assignments do not facilitate good study habits, and many times actually promote bad ones. Junior high school students should not be assigned homework that has already been mastered at school or homework which would require teacher supervision.

Independent study materials must be based on new knowledge and concepts developed through research concerning the learning process.

> Programmed material that divides the complex subject into small logical steps, giving the student the correct answer to each step immediately after he has written his own answer, and research projects for the able pupils facilitate good study habits during independent study. Psychologists have found that students or trainees using programmed teaching materials can master complex materials in one-half to two-thirds the time required by the conventional teaching methods.[4]

4. Some widely accepted growth and developmental characteristics of the preadolescent would indicate a need for a quality independent study program at the junior high school level. The youngster is striving to become an independent individual and needs to make decisions and accept responsibility. The pupil must develop self-discipline and make generalizations and comparisons. Self-control, time management, and decision-making by the pupil are not taught by lecturing or completing questions in a workbook but by allowing the pupil freedom to develop those traits through experiencing them. Junior high school pupils participating in independent study have found it to be a powerful motivating and stimulating situation. A parent of a ninth grade student involved in mathematics

programmed instruction at Brookhurst Junior High School called the school because she felt it was not right for her fifteen-year-old boy to study mathematics on Christmas Day. Her son was highly motivated and had established his own goals and objectives in mathematics; he felt an urgency to study mathematics even though it was Christmas. The mother was assured that such behavior on her son's part, while unusual, was not necessarily unfortunate, and she was convinced by the school that the teacher did not assign homework to her son. He was one of the pupils in the independent study program in mathematics and had established his own goals and homework assignments.

6. Independent study can provide a quality education for pupils in special education. Programmed instruction is an efficient technique of maximizing the effectiveness of traditional techniques of instruction for the deaf and hard of hearing.

> Programmed instruction is by no means a substitute for conventional instruction by the teacher but a complement to it. Independent study clearly needs professional teacher supervision. Programmed instruction does hold the promise of contributing substantially to more effective written communication.[5]

7. Independent study will facilitate greater use of automatic devices to perform all or part of a considerable number of teaching activities. An analysis of the technological aids to decide which is to be used for a given purpose, i.e., when to use television, overhead projectors, records, films, slides, tapes, and other instruments. The latest scientific advances can be implemented into the independent study laboratories. Programmed teaching is based on new knowledge and concepts developed through research concerning the learning process.

8. Junior high school pupils need an area in the school where they can be alone to think and study without the usual school interruptions. If a pupil has been absent, he needs enough flexibility in his daily schedule as well as the physical environment to catch up with his studies. He needs physical space devoid of interruptions—a place where he can be alone and free to contemplate his future and present. Also, areas are needed that contain those books, instruments, and other tools of learning so necessary in the development of good study habits and self-discipline.

Many of today's schools make only gestures toward providing a learning environment where the objectives of independent study can be realized. The self-contained classrooms, single track programs, rigid grade organizations, and inflexible schedules do not allow for maximum individual attainment, development of self-control, and increased motivation.

A New Structure Needed for Independent Study in the Dynamic Junior High School Program

The need for and importance of independent study for the junior high school pupil is seldom challenged. However, the type of educational structure that will assist a functional program of independent study cannot be found in the traditional framework so often met with in the junior high school. Three basic changes necessary in the modern junior high school structure to facilitate effective independent study programs are:

First, the schedule must have time and number flexibility. Teachers must be able to control their daily schedules, and pupils must be given some responsibility in determining their independent study time. The responsibility for the use of time is placed on students and teachers rather than on standardized policies operating in the principal's office. The policies of the junior high school should be directed toward increasing pupil responsibility. The student who is to participate in an individual study program must be freed from the lockstep procedures which are so common in the rigid program of the junior high school. Most junior high school teachers have experienced the frustration of spending many laborious hours to prepare a well-developed lesson plan appropriate for the group and then to find the learning pace is inappropriate for individuals within the group. A program that permits the student the freedom of scheduling a program of independent study will be flexible enough to meet the individual learning requirements of the student. The following activities that occur in individual study can best take place within a flexible schedule: reading, listening to records and tapes, reviewing, inquiring, analyzing, thinking, experimenting, examining, investigating, writing, creating, memorizing, recording, constructing, and self-appraising.

Second, the faculty of the dynamic junior high school must understand the nature of independent study and the flexible schedule, then they must realize its implications to learning for the junior high school pupil. They must know the purposes and the uses of small-group discussion, large-group classes, and their role in a program of individual study.

Third, the school plant and educational facilities must be so constructed and arranged that they facilitate the independent study needs of the students, i.e., individual study carrels, well-equipped laboratories, and programmed learning areas. Specific learning tasks require an area for doing individual study, for working on laboratory projects, and for doing learning programs.

The content of independent study and programmed material must be planned to include a logical, developmental sequence of daily learning activities and experiences whereby pupils may make steady and consistent progress toward planned goals and objectives. The independent study programs must be integrated into a planned program as defined by the District course of study, the Board of Education requirements, and the State curriculum policies.

A brief explanation of the development and implementation of a course of study is necessary to understand the relationship of content to an independent study program. The origin of a course of study usually involves three contributors—the teachers, the local community, and the State. Curriculum committees, composed of teachers who work in summer workshops, draft the course of study based upon the requisites and needs of the local community and the requirements of the State Board of Education. District and university consultants many times work directly with the various teacher committees writing the course of study. After approval by the administrators, the superintendent, and the Board of Education, the course of study becomes District policy. See Figure One.

The various courses of study are then presented to the department chairmen at the building level where the teachers enrich and supplement the course of study through the development of resource units. At this point the various teaching teams decide what concept of the resource unit should be taught, whether to use large-group techniques, small-group discussion, or independent study. By checking the Curriculum Flow Chart, Figure One, the teaching teams at

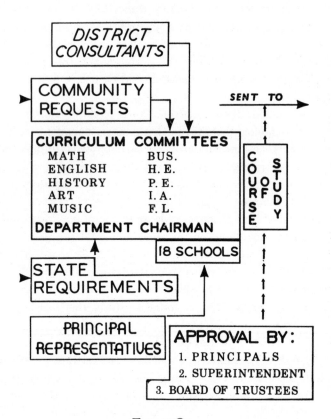

FIGURE ONE

Brookhurst Junior High School in Anaheim, California, decided that the following would constitute programmed instruction and independent study:

1. General Mathematics, Algebra I, Geometry, and Algebra II through the use of the Temac material.
2. English Grammar through the use of the 2600 and 3200 series by Blumenthal, published by Harcourt Brace.
3. Elective contract subjects such as Homemaking, Industrial Arts, Speech, Drama, Journalism, Arts and Crafts, and Typing.
4. Living World History research projects.
5. Ninth grade science projects—the basic content taught in large- and small-group techniques.

6. Foreign Language laboratories where the student could hear tapes and practice conversing in the new language via the tape recorder.

Prior to entering a program of independent study, each pupil should be interviewed and tested; parents should be contacted regarding the needs and interests of their youngster. Counselors determine and compile basic information necessary for placement; however, they do not place pupils in the various independent study programs. The data accumulated on the pupil by the counselor are related to the teaching team leaders who make the decisions regarding placement in subjects, ability groups, and independent study. The rational for placement of a pupil in programmed instruction and independent study is based upon a multitude of characteristics. The one characteristic that each pupil must possess is self-reliance and the ability to work independently of direct adult supervision. A daily review of the student's progress in each of the programmed instructional areas is made by a member of the teaching team or the student's scheduling advisor. If it is determined that the student is learning the concept and accomplishing the established objectives of the course, credit is earned. However, if test results indicate a lack of pupil self-discipline, he is returned to the developmental stages of the specific program. See Figure One. The student is placed with a teaching team where there is more direct supervision and guidance by the teachers. Usually the number of students not responding to the independent study program is extremely small—five or six pupils per year in each of the programmed subject areas.

One of the chief results of independent study is that the teacher becomes dispensable rather than indispensable to pupils. After reaching a primary objective in the programmed instruction, pupils merely report to a clerical aide for a copy of the examination. They complete the test, return it to the clerical aide, and immediately proceed to the next concept to be learned. The test paper is corrected and submitted to the teaching team for evaluation in light of the student's ability and goals.

In the junior high school pupils are able to handle and make effective use of the freedom given them through independent study. Pupils achieve far beyond the objectives they would have realized in a traditional classroom environment. Those pupils participating in the independent study programs have demonstrated achievement in depth and enrichment as well as the quantity of subject matter covered. There appears to be horizontal movements through the subject as well as vertical coverage. At Brookhurst Junior High School in the study of Nationalism, Imperialism, and Mercantilism, the pupils in the World History independent study program studied in depth to the extent that some students were recognized as specialists on their particular topics and were used as consultants by the teachers. Recognition of and success for the pupils in the independent study program contributed more fuel to motivation already highly fired. In addition to the phenomenon of working algebra on Christmas Day, came a request by pupils in World History to open the school library three nights a week from seven to nine in the evening. Teachers petitioned the administration for library keys in order to satisfy the newly found appetites for learning of pupils.

Let's Get Going

How and where to start in the development of an independent study program at the junior high school level is always of concern to the school administrator. The Board of Education could begin by constructing or remodeling a school plant to incorporate the modern concepts of study carrels, electronic programmed devices, and facilities for large- and small-group teaching techniques. Another point of departure would constitute the training and accumulating of a faculty dedicated to improvement of the quality of junior high school education. Still another starting point would be to alter the basic structure of the school day to provide a flexible schedule. Innovating schools throughout the nation have either started from one of the above-mentioned points or a combination of the three. Eventually all three projects—modern school plant and facilities, innovating faculty, and a flexible schedule—must be realized before full utilization can be made of a functional independent study program.

It is unimportant at this time to suggest the best point of departure; however, Brookhurst Junior High School in the Anaheim Union High School District chose the latter, the development of a flexible schedule, a schedule that would give to the faculty and students flexibility in time, space, number, and facility. After a three-year struggle, the school has a vehicle that allows complete and unobstructed flexibility for pupils, teacher, and subjects. The teachers are now embarked on project two, the job of learning how to make optimum use of the vehicle of flexibility. The traditional Brookhurst school plant places severe handicaps not only upon the program of flexible scheduling but also upon the independent study program. Without a humanities laboratory, a science laboratory, and a spacious and functional library, as well as other physical facilities, the program is not operating as effectively as it might. The full potential of an independent study program conducted in a traditional plant cannot be evaluated with validity.

The basic structure of the flexible schedule and the independent study program of Brookhurst Junior High School makes the following assumptions:

1. A performance criteria of students rather than a time criteria to determine the type of activity the teacher plans for her students is essential.
2. Teachers and teaching teams determine time, need, size of study group, facility, and methodology for each day of school. A new master schedule based upon teacher requests is developed each day; therefore, there are never two master schedules identical in any school year.
3. With the assistance of counselors, teachers define pupil needs and program for various achievement levels continuously throughout the school year.
4. Students make the choice of determining their daily schedules.
5. Students select electives on a contract basis and are not required to attend these classes every day. Courses labeled as contract electives are conducted as individual study except when the teacher needs to order a large group for lecture to explain concepts that would be common to all students even though they are developing different projects, i.e., principles of safety in the operation of a new electric saw in woodshop.
6. Students have the option to accept or reject tutoring opportunities which are in addition to regular classes required each day, such as mathematics, English, World History, and foreign language and physical education.
7. Teachers may excuse students from certain class activities or for

the complete course when they feel that independent study and research are more beneficial to the students.

8. The criteria for selection of students placed in independent study programs are determined by the teacher on the basis of self-reliance, motivation, and study habits.

The Brookhurst Flexible Scheduling Program has incorporated the above-mentioned assumptions. The program involves all of the four hundred thirty-five students at the ninth grade level; however, the seventh and eighth grades are organized on a seven-period day and are not part of the program. The faculty in the program is organized into teaching teams of subject areas, i.e., the Mathematics and Science Team, the Language Arts Team, and the History Team. The teachers' job orders are coordinated in the principal's office and the schedule changes are made there.

The individual teachers, teaching teams, counselors, and administrators submit job orders daily. The job orders (see Figure Two) are requests for periods of time, total number of students desired, size of groups, facility needed, and additional clerical or faculty as-

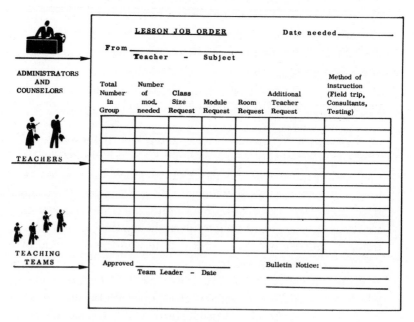

FIGURE TWO

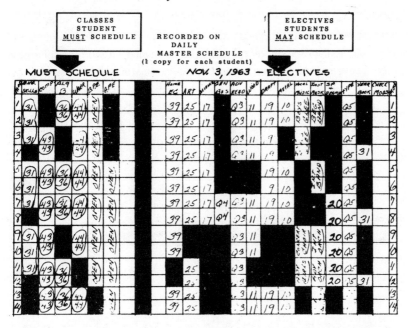

FIGURE THREE

sistance. A daily master schedule (see Figure Three) is constructed from the job orders submitted by the faculty four days prior to the day it becomes operational.

The students schedule a fourteen-modular day from materials

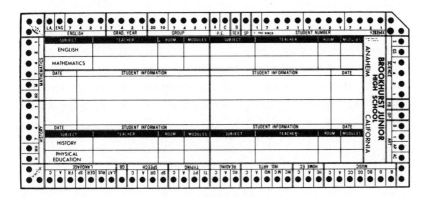

FIGURE FOUR

derived from the master schedule. Students meet with a scheduling advisor before school begins each morning to process their schedules. With the assistance of the advisor, they complete a student schedule (see Figure Four) based upon the daily master schedule for three days hence and pick up the schedule that becomes operational that particular day. On the day after the students have completed a schedule, a class roll, derived from tickets torn from the completed student's schedule (see Figure Five) is given to the teachers. The

FIGURE FIVE

above-mentioned process is repeated each day throughout the year, and an entirely new master schedule is produced; the schedule based upon job orders by the teachers is produced.

The program allows teachers to determine the time needed for each instructional unit as well as the method of instruction and the school facility best suited to the lesson. Students' schedules are changed daily as the teachers' plans change the master schedule. The program encourages students to utilize the independent study areas and the contract electives through the scheduling process. A teaching team demands the time of a student or group of students for a particular day and indicates this demand through the use of the office master schedule (see Figure Six). Only the modules demanded by the teachers will appear on the student's schedule (see Figure Seven); therefore, there will be modules during the day that will be available to the student for independent study and contract electives (see Figure Eight). The student chooses the contract electives and

FIGURE SIX

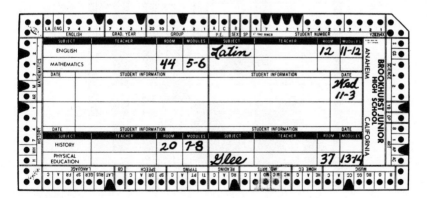

FIGURE SEVEN

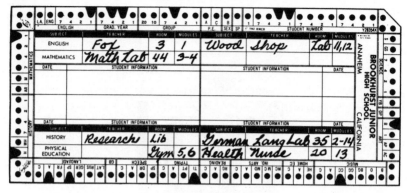

FIGURE EIGHT

independent study time from the elective master schedule (see Figure Nine) which is made up from those offerings by the teachers. The independent study areas, library, laboratories, and contract electives' classrooms are open during most of the fourteen modules in order that students scheduling themselves during their free time can utilize those facilities.

FIGURE NINE

The Brookhurst Flexible Scheduling Program is essentially a performance schedule of the individual student. The program does not operate on the basis of a static grouping of youngsters but upon the needs of the individual student. The teacher can call different size groups on the basis of actual student performance in class. Different rates of growth can be accommodated through individual tutoring; or when a number of particular students are identified by the teacher, a special class can be scheduled. Students who are having difficulty with a particular class may be required to spend additional time in class. Interested or designated students can be grouped together for special types of activity, for independent study, or for research; or they can progress to more demanding forms of subject matter. Teachers may make use of free time by scheduling students for conferences or tutoring on an individual basis. The teacher may make this either optional or required for the student. Teachers have found this much more effective as a long-term technique than requiring the student to report after school for individual help, make-up, or conference.

The responsibility of the student in making out his own schedule is carefully structured and controlled. The student must honor all academic classes required by teachers before scheduling his choices from other areas. All fourteen modules must be accounted for. See Figure Ten. Students may schedule themselves for programmed instruction, counseling, assemblies, testing, electives, independent study, tutoring, field trips, and special events such as outside speakers.

FIGURE TEN

The Contract Elective and Independent Study

The contract elective is most universally utilized as independent study by junior high school pupils. In many elective areas the students and teacher make an agreement that a certain amount of credit will be granted upon the satisfactory completion of a project. The projects differ in complexity and interest. The student does not have to report everyday, nor is there a time limit placed upon completion of the project. The elective shop teacher may require attendance in a large group until he is satisfied that the student is proficient in the handling of tools and is observant of good safety rules. The acceptance by the teacher of a student contract presupposes that the student has met certain requirements and standards.

The Contract Elective Agreement Form (see Figure Eleven) in-

ELECTIVE AGREEMENT

_____Elective Project

Student's Name:_____ Date:_____

Group Counselor's Name:_____

DESCRIPTION OF PROJECT:

_____

_____

_____Prerequisites (if any):_____

Routing	Signature
Project teacher approves the contract and gives to student to sign:	_____
	(student)
Student takes project home for parent okay	_____
	(parent)
Student brings contract to group counselor who records the information:	_____
	(group counselor)
Group counselor places contract in project teacher's box.	_____
	(project teacher)

FIGURE ELEVEN

cludes the name of the student, date, scheduling counselor, description of the project, and parent's, and project teacher's signatures. The contract agreement is then filed by the project teacher until the pupil either satisfactorily completes the project with credit earned or drops the project because of some unforeseen reason. After completion of his project, the student may draft another contract in the same subject area or choose another elective on the basis of exploration or interest.

The junior high school has been relieved of the responsibility of giving definite vocational training and is no longer considered as the educational terminus for a large group of early adolescents. The purpose of exploration as a junior high school objective is a real and meaningful goal.

> To lead pupils to discover and explore their specialized interest, aptitudes, and abilities as a basis for decisions regarding educational opportunities. To lead pupils to discover and explore their specialized interest, aptitudes, and abilities as a basis for present and future vocational decisions. To stimulate pupils and provide opportunities for them to develop a continually widening range of cultural, social, civic, avocational, and recreational interests.[9]

Pupils in the Brookhurst Program through independent study and the contract agreement plan may explore every subject area of the school curriculum sometime during the school year. Many students participate in as many as four or five different electives during their ninth grade year.

An example of a student's transcript for the first semester of the ninth grade is shown below.

	PUPIL No. 1	1/24/64	
Courses		Grade	Semester Hours
Physical Education		B	5
English I—College Prep		A	5
Algebra I		A	5
French I		A	5
Latin I		A	5
Russian I		A	5
Reading, Advanced		B	5
World History		A	5
Glee Club		A	5

The transcript for pupil No. 1 indicates nine courses, five of which are elective subjects. This pupil has a special interest in foreign languages; therefore, because of the flexible schedule and independent study, he is able to register for three different foreign languages. In a typical ninth grade program at least two of the courses would be eliminated.

PUPIL No. 2	1/24/64	
Courses	*Grade*	*Semester Hours*
Physical Education	A	5
English—College Prep	B	5
Science I	B	5
German I	B	5
Algebra I	A	5
Geometry I	A	5
Office Practice	B	5
Drama	B	5
World History—College	A	5

Pupil No. 2 was assigned to independent study in the mathematics programmed instructional laboratory where he was able to complete Algebra I and Geometry I in one semester. By taking advantage of the flexible scheduling, the pupil utilized Flexible Scheduling to pursue an extensive study in mathematics in accordance with his individual interests and talents. At the same time he earned credit in four elective subjects, one of them a foreign language.

PUPIL No. 3	1/24/64	
Courses	*Grade*	*Semester Hours*
Physical Education	D	5
English I—Non-College Prep	D	5
General Mathematics	D	5
World History	D	5
Remedial Reading	D	5

Pupil No. 3 is scheduling himself into the reading laboratory. Until he is reading at ability level, he will schedule himself into many modules each day in Remedial Reading. In a rigid seven-period day, frustrating and montonous failure encountered in a rigid scheduling school would more than likely produce another dropout. The elective subjects do not become a haven or a dumping ground for the student failing in the academic subjects. A diagnosis of the student's deficiency is made, and the remedial student is scheduled daily into a counselor-pupil conceived program of basic and remedial education.

The traditional procedure of preregistration in the spring of the year is not necessary in the Brookhurst Program. A new elective contract can be selected anytime during the school year. At the same time, students do not need to wait for the end of a semester in order to drop or complete an elective subject. During the second day of school in September, the teachers of the elective subjects present to all the pupils in the ninth grade the overview, objectives, activities, and projects of their particular subjects. The purpose of the orientation by the elective teachers is to give the pupils an opportunity to make intelligent and enlightened decisions regarding their choice of electives. To require an eighth grade student to choose between General Business or Journalism in March many times results in a request for a program change before November of the next school year. New courses can be started at any time and old ones dropped. Students' needs and interests do not always coincide with the beginning and ending of semesters.

Students have demonstrated repeatedly that they can learn much more through contemplation and through individual research. In addition, they have demonstrated that the pace of learning which is appropriate for a group is often inappropriate for each individual within the group. The teacher must direct, organize, and supervise the independent study area that will permit a pupil to pursue an idea, an experiment, a problem, or a project. Teachers present projects that allow a pupil in individual study an opportunity to analyze, to synthesize, to judge, to imagine, to contemplate, and to create additional projects. Flexible scheduling and independent study affect the role of the teacher; therefore, junior high school teacher-reactions become desirable in the discussion of independent study in the junior high school.

Mrs. Bea Grodahl, homemaking teacher at Brookhurst Junior High School, states,

> Flexible scheduling has offered many opportunities for more desirable teaching and learning situations in homemaking, especially through the use of independent study.

I feel that being able to designate the amount of time (continuous modules) for a specific activity is one of the greatest contributions of flexible scheduling to the homemaking program. The food and nutrition area, especially, is more enjoyable for both students and teacher. The students' performance in this area is more desirable because ample time may be allotted to satisfactorily complete a project. Being able to designate class size according to facilities and equipment allows for more efficient use of time by the student; this is especially true in the clothing construction area.

The teacher has an opportunity to work with a larger cross-section of the student body because the more able students may carry more electives under this program than under a rigid schedule. There has been a forty percent increase in enrollment in homemaking under this program.

Because the student has been given some freedom in deciding the number of modules that she wishes to spend in homemaking, she appears to have accepted more responsibility and developed a more business-like attitude toward her work. More enthusiasm in the projects has been observed.

The small group sessions and independent study provide an opportunity for the teacher to know and understand the students as well as to establish a closer relationship with them. I feel that this program has given greater self-satisfaction to both students and teachers.

Mr. David Loop, art teacher at Brookhurst, states,

I have found flexible scheduling more advantageous than rigid scheduling in the art department for two primary reasons: First, with flexible scheduling the student may spend more time in class. This enables the student to work on his art project for a prolonged period of time rather than hurrying to get out supplies, work for a short time, and then cleanup as is practiced under rigid scheduling. Second, the teacher may work for an entire day, more or less, with a special group of students on a special project without having all the art students on that same day. For example, our art department cooperates with the music and drama departments in presenting our annual Christmas Program. On certain days I would schedule just my art program committee to work on the scenery construction in an independent project situation. I had no other students scheduled; on these days the other art students scheduled themselves in other subjects, and I met with just the special group. At the same time those students who worked in the independent project over a long period of time did not miss any academic courses. Therefore, the English and mathematics teachers were not unhappy with the art department as they were formerly in a rigid schedule when these students were pulled from their academic classes.

Mr. Norman Visca explains further advantages of independent study in the industrial arts department,

> In the industrial arts area, flexible scheduling offers many distinct advantages which a rigid program cannot. The contract agreement is completed by the student in order to receive credit and allows the student to progress at his own desired rate. A student can spend as much time in industrial arts as his schedule permits, thus affording him opportunity to gain broader skills and knowledge. Also, he may fulfill his contract in a short period of time which allows him to sign a new agreement for additional credit or go to new elective areas. The academically inclined student is afforded time in industrial arts that a static program cannot afford. By using time in a more flexible way all the students have an opportunity to take industrial arts.

At Brookhurst teachers of the remedial or slow student agree that individual study activities present the greatest opportunities for individualizing instructional offerings. Independent study and programmed instruction assignments of many types, whether pupil or teacher initiated, can satisfy the intellectual needs and interests of the low-ability pupils.

Some Obvious and Some Subtle Changes through Independent Study

The evaluation model of a junior high school with a design of independent study, programmed learning, flexible scheduling, and team teaching is comprehensive and complex. Drastic reorganization of the basic education program will require an evaluation which differs from those typically used in today's testing scheme. A new group of educational goals must be included with the traditional objectives. Creative thinking, problem solving, self-reliance and control, and research techniques must be included with the measurement of subject matter. For example, an evaluation that includes the number of resource and library books circulating from the library is as important as determining the reading achievement in the evaluation of a remedial and developmental reading program. An evaluation that determines the creative ability of pupils must be included along with tests that measure memorization of facts.

There are some immediate and obvious changes that can be felt, seen, and measured soon after innovations begin. Independent study programs are organized specifically for greater fulfillment of the potential capacity of each junior high school pupil. The school library assumes a new and important role in the total picture of the educational program. Library books begin to circulate at an astonishing rate; in the Brookhurst library the circulation tripled during the second year of the program.

The pupil's selection of an educational program is no longer restricted by time as in a rigid school day. Through the use of independent study in a flexible program, a junior high school can offer many additional courses, not only in foreign language—Brookhurst has five—but additional courses in all subject areas. The enrollment in the elective courses has doubled since the inception of the independent study program at Brookhurst.

Attendance and self-discipline seem to improve in direct relationship with the amount of increased freedom given to pupils in planning their schedules. Independent study has helped dropout students to stay in school. Since the beginning of independent study at Brookhurst, not one ninth grade pupil has dropped out of school.

Independent study and flexible scheduling in an educational program meet the needs of the individual students rather than forcing the pupil to meet the rigid artificial demands of the school. Independent study programs stimulate inquiry by the student rather than the acceptance by the student of answers from the teacher. This spirit of inquiry, fostered by and nurtured by the various independent study programs, has been due to a program which establishes the right of self-determination by the student.

CHAPTER 7

Senior High School Uses of Flexible Programming in Independent Study

by

JAY W. FORMSMA

Prior to becoming principal of the high school at Livonia, Michigan, Jay W. Formsma was principal of Holland High School in that state. While he was at Holland, the staff developed a program emphasizing independent study. He received his master's degree from the University of Michigan and has done graduate work at Michigan State University.

LET US TAKE a look at some representative statements of school philosophy. Probably the following compares readily to most school philosophies.

A. We conceive the function of the school system to be that of educating all the children of all the people to live successfully in a democracy.

B. It is our purpose to create an environment in which each individual is prepared by experience to take his place of responsibility in a democratic society.

C. Our country is dedicated to the ideal of democracy as a way of human life. We, therefore, believe that the education program should promote and perpetuate by precept and practice this democratic ideal in which the school is engaged so that each individual may develop the abilities and characteristics essential to effective social living in a democratic society.

D. We recognize each child as an individual who needs to be understood, respected and loved, in order that he may have a feeling of security as a member of the group.

E. We believe that each pupil should be given the opportunity to grow according to his varying interests, needs, abilities, and capacity for learning.

Further focus can be added by two statements from "Education For Freedom and World Understanding," a publication of the United States Office of Education.

F. "The central issue of our day is human freedom, and the crux of freedom is the right of individual choice."

G. "Freedom of action has necessary limits, but freedom of expression must not be denied, even to those on the left and on the right."

The critics of the secondary schools have bases for attack. We are not doing the job we have described for ourselves in our written philosophies. We become very defensive and run to our professional and accrediting associations when the critics point their finger and say, "thou lackest here."

The Folklore of Education

In our culture we find it difficult to understand the Hindu. He will worship a sacred cow—nurture and feed him—while at the same moment people about him may be starving to death. We would say that he should consider a cow to be a cow and nothing more. Yet with all our enlightenment, we have a few sacred cows in our culture. Indeed, our education world is full of them. Our sacred cows are many and varied. These sacred cows in education may well be preventing us from achieving our objectives. Each time we eliminate a sacred cow from our prerequisites we find a great degree of freedom within which to plan our programs.

SACRED COW: ALL CLASSES SHOULD BE FIFTY-FIVE
MINUTES IN LENGTH

This device provides a convenient way for the administrator to establish a framework within which all teachers and students must live and learn. This is not representative of life. The only time in an individual's life that he will experience this arrangement of time is from grades seven through twelve. It is artificial. It does not prepare him for adult life or work. It appears to be a device used to reduce enrollments in the junior and senior high schools. If a student cannot survive this regimental device, he is removed from the school population.

Administration and faculty then point with pride to this device of selection which they assume guarantees quality in education. No concern is paid to the fact that they are not meeting the objectives that schools have set for themselves in their philosophies in terms of "meeting the needs of all the children of all of the people."

Many class activities take more than fifty-five minutes; some take less. Some class activities take a good deal of time to prepare or to clean up the working area. Why not tailor the time to the concept or the activity the teachers feel must be taught? It is a more sensible approach to allow the nature of the material at hand to determine the adding, subtracting, multiplying, or dividing of the school day into instructional units of time. It makes more sense to allow the teacher to select the amount of time needed for a particular concept to be taught. Let us give some control of time back to the classroom teacher.

SACRED COW: ALL CLASSES SHOULD CONTAIN
TWENTY-FIVE STUDENTS AND ONE TEACHER

New methods which have investigated instruction in various size student groups have shown much success. Many schools across the country have objective data to verify these results.

There are many kinds of instruction that can go on in large groups. The alert teacher and administrator see quickly the opportunities within such a plan. Through careful planning it is possible to provide teaching situations in which teachers can save time by grouping students in large groups for those activities which lend themselves to this method. This saved time can then be used in individual conferences, lesson preparation, marking of tests, and other school business.

SACRED COW: ALL STUDENTS MUST BE IN SCHOOL
AND UNDER SUPERVISION ALL DAY, EVERY DAY

In the name of education this does not have to exist. It may have to exist because parents want the schools to babysit, students have to be transported thirty miles from home to school, or some restrictive department of public instruction requires students to be in school from 8:30 until 3:30, regardless of the implications for quality education. But it is not necessary to all secondary education. Some schools may not be able to take advantage of this freedom to a full extent. Modifications can be employed. For those who are willing to sacrifice this sacred cow, great returns in terms of student achievement and individual responsibilities will result.

SACRED COW: STUDY HALLS ARE ESSENTIAL TO THE
OPERATION OF A SECONDARY SCHOOL

A corollary might be, study halls are a necessary evil in the operation of the secondary schools.

Study halls are places to keep students under maximum security while they wait for another class to begin. Administrators have sold them under many names—study halls, independent resource centers, learning laboratories. In truth study halls are maximum security detention areas from which students may not escape unless they have passes signed by two guards which they must be able to produce at strategically located check points. The faculty in charge are violently opposed to study halls. Parents recognize them as inefficient, yet we still operate them and point with pride to them.

We feel that fifty percent of our discipline problems were eliminated when we eliminated the study hall. I have heard many principals subscribe to the adage, "As the study hall goes, so goes the classroom." We no longer live in dread of the study halls the day of the big game. We no longer have to be alert to the problems of the last study hall before vacation or, worse still, admit defeat and send the last hour study hall home.

SACRED COW: LEARNING TAKES PLACE ONLY AS
A FACULTY MEMBER DIRECTS THE STUDENT
IN CLASS OR IN ASSIGNED DRILL WORK

This sacred cow negates the old maxim that experience is the best teacher. Students can and do learn on their own initiative. At times I believe they learn in spite of us, not because of us. This sacred cow is based on the old concept that the teacher is the only source of knowledge and truth and that the teacher dispenses to the student that body of knowledge that the teacher deems necessary and good at a particular time.

New techniques developed with new teaching aids make it possible for students to learn with a minimum of supervision. We have also learned that students can help each other through discussion activities and smaller seminar groups. We have found that it is not necessary for a student to do all his learning directly under the eye of a teacher.

Then, too, there are some faculty and parents who refuse to accept the fact that the children know more than they do about certain areas of knowledge. The children must have gotten it somehow without the help of the teacher. We have not tapped this huge reservoir of potential instructors.

SACRED COW: ALL STUDENTS HAVE THE SAME NEEDS,
SAME SKILLS, SAME PREPARATION, SAME CAPACITY,
SAME MOTIVATIONS, AND SAME OBJECTIVES

We are working with individuals and must cultivate, water, nurture each one so that he will grow at his maximum growth rate. This means that we must grant students the necessary freedom of time to supplement the regular instructional program. It means that not all students will have to cover all phases of a particular subject-matter area. It is foolhardy and inefficient to force students through units of work they have previously understood. The teacher must then become a skilled supervisor and librarian, directing a program with the student. They plan this program which complements and supplements the student's previous knowledge. At all cost, they must avoid being forced through previously learned material.

It is about time we roast our "sacred cows" in an effort to nourish our educational program. Of course, in dispensing with our "sacred cows" we must be careful not to brush aside the conventional just to be unconventional. We must also be careful that the solutions to our present problems do not become new "sacred cows." What we must recognize in making the transition from the old to the new is that our present education was molded for another age, not the one in which we live. We must match this insight with creative new patterns which will correspond to the strange and quick-changing movements of our time.

New Needs Demand New Programs

We must meet the challenge of a tomorrow with a far greater body of knowledge. The tempo of living has been shattered by innovations of tremendous impact. To fit the present age, to meet its problems, to evaluate its responsibilities and to accept them calls for a new process of education that brings the high school student maturity as well as knowledge.

Our problem, indeed the problem of every culture of every age, is to build a more responsible citizenry. Independence and responsibility are learned, not earned. Our democracy has survived in spite of the rigid, dictatorial program of our schools. Freedom and responsibility are like a two-sided coin. Freedom is one side, responsibility the other.

We had better do something about this problem. The coming of age in the United States is high school graduation. After this point students are given freedom. They are not restricted. As evidence of our failure to build into our students responsibility, I submit graduation night—a night of deepest concern for administrators, teachers, and parents.

We must devise ways of granting students freedom and responsibility. One way which is showing great promise is the move toward independent study in the high schools.

New Concepts and Old Ideas

Independent study is a relatively new concept to most school people. There is undoubtedly some confusion about what it is. A distinction should be made at this point about the difference between independent study and individual study. Independent study indicates that the student is probably working on his own time, in his own direction, with occasional guidance from a teacher. Individual study may well be done by the teacher describing the problem and the whole class responding to the problem as individuals. The difference might well be noted in the names themselves—"independent" would mean not dependent upon the teacher or upon class work. "Individual" study would probably be dependent upon both. Individual study would include help on daily work, make-up work, make-up tests, additional help needed for weak students and remedial work. The difference between independent study and individual study might be explained by pointing out that individual study might well be done during the class period and independent study would not. Independent study, not dependent upon class work, would almost always be done outside of class time. Plans for independent study would vary, depending on the student, teacher, resources available, and the subject area.

A tentative plan for independent study might be:

Step 1. Approval of the project by the subject-matter department of the school.

Step 2. Presentation of a written plan to be approved by the department. This would include:

A. Theses to be investigated.

B. Resource, research, and bibliography of materials available.

C. Methods to be employed.

D. Materials to be used.

Step 3. Progress report to committee chairman (six-week intervals).

Step 4. Oral examination by departmental committee. (At least three teachers and community resource people.)

Step 5. Written examination to be evaluated by department.

Step 6. Public presentation of project report.

The amount of credit to be granted for the project would be determined by departmental committee and would be recommended to principal for approval.

To achieve either independent study or individual study two things are required within the schedule. First, time must be provided for the student so that he can work independently of other students and teachers. Second, time must be provided for faculty so that they can have frequent conferences with students who are working independently. Both faculty and students must have time when both are free of other class assignments so that they can meet and work together. Any schedule that is constructed to implement independent or individual study must contain these two components.

Another important decision must be made before the schedule is planned. Are students going to be contained, or are students to have some freedom of movement? My experience seems to indicate that it will be one or the other. Either you contain the student body, or you allow them freedom. There seems to be no half-way ground.

The Schedule Sets the Limits

Schedules can have greater or lesser numbers of "sacred cows." The program with the fewer number of "sacred cows" will have the greater opportunity for success. However, it is not necessary to incorporate all the innovations that have been successful in other school situations. Many schools have done extremely well on one concept and have not made changes in others. Each faculty member and administrator must make his own decisions on these things. The program of a particular school cannot and should not be moved completely into another school and community. Each faculty must develop its own program for its own school and community.

Models Presented

There are about four directions that secondary school programs can take.

1. The high school program can continue as it has in the past. No particular comment will be made on the traditional secondary school program. The following is an example of a student's schedule:

Time	Monday	Tuesday	Wednesday	Thursday	Friday
8:30	Chemistry	Chemistry	Chemistry	Chemistry	Chemistry
9:30	Study	Study	Study	Study	Study
10:30	English	English	English	English	English
	L	U	N	C	H
12:30	Math	Math	Math	Math	Math
1:30	Physical Education	Physical Education	Physical Education	Physical Education	Physical Education
2:30	U.S. History	U.S. History	U.S. History	U.S. History	U.S. History

TRADITIONAL STUDENT SCHEDULE

The following is an example of a teacher's schedule:

Time	Monday	Tuesday	Wednesday	Thursday	Friday
8:30	U.S. History	U.S. History	U.S. History	U.S. History	U.S. History
9:30	World History	World History	World History	World History	World History
10:30	U.S. History	U.S. History	U.S. History	U.S. History	U.S. History
	L	U	N	C	H
12:30	Conference Period	Conference Period	Conference Period	Conference Period	Conference Period
1:30	World History	World History	World History	World History	World History
2:30	U.S. History	U.S. History	U.S. History	U.S. History	U.S. History

TRADITIONAL TEACHER SCHEDULE

2. The class periods can be shortened to fifteen- or twenty-minute modules. Usually nineteen to twenty-four modules are contained in the school day. The modules can then be blocked together back to back to provide any length of time desired:

         1 period—15 minutes
         3 periods—45 minutes
         6 periods—90 minutes

Usually the schedule is set once a year and continued throughout the year.

This type of schedule provides a more varied schedule. It is possible to provide for any time sequence; but once it is set, it is rather difficult to change without affecting other faculty members and students. This type of schedule usually develops so that students have small segments of time (fifteen minutes) not used for instruction. These small segments of time are rather difficult for students to use effectively. The following is an example of a student's schedule:

Time	Monday	Tuesday	Wednesday	Thursday	Friday
8:20	English–History L.G.		History L.G.	English–History L.G.	
9:20	English–History Lab.	Math L.G.	Math Seminar	English–History Lab.	Math L.G.
					Typing
10:20	Chemistry L.G.	Typing Lab.	Chemistry L.G.	Chemistry L.G.	Typing Lab.
	L	U	N	C	H
11:20	French L.G.		Science Seminar	French L.G.	
12:20	Physical Education Lab.	Physical Education Lab.	Physical Education L.G.	Physical Education Lab.	Physical Education Lab.
1:20	French Seminar	Chemistry Lab.	French Seminar	French Seminar	Chemistry Lab.
2:20	Math Lab.	History Seminar		Math Lab.	English Seminar

L.G.—Large Group

INDIVIDUAL STUDENT SCHEDULE

(20-minute module)

Ridgewood High School, Norridge, Illinois

The following is an example of a teacher's schedule:

Time	Monday	Tuesday	Wednesday	Thursday	Friday
8:20	English-History L.G.°		History L.G.	English-History L.G.°	
9:20	English-History Lab.	History Seminar / History Seminar		English-History Lab.	History Seminar / History Seminar
10:20	English-History Lab.	English-History Lab.	H.R.C. / N	English-History Lab.	English-History Lab.
11:20	L / History Seminar	U / English-History Lab.		C / History Seminar	H / English-History Lab.
12:20	History Seminar	English-History Lab.		History Seminar	English-History Lab.
1:20	H.R.C.			H.R.C.	
2:20	History Seminar	History Seminar		History Seminar	History Seminar

°—Second Person
H.R.C.—Humanities Resource Center
L.G.—Large Group

INDIVIDUAL HISTORY TEACHER SCHEDULE
(20-minute module)
Ridgewood High School, Norridge, Illinois

3. The class period can be lengthened. Longer blocks of time can be used. The example used here is one hundred and five minutes. The

day is divided into four periods. These classes meet three times per week. Thus the faculty member has freedom to vary the instruction within this block of time. If twenty minutes are needed for a particular concept to be taught, twenty minutes are used. If sixty minutes are needed, they are used. This system allows the teacher to select time segments as needed for instruction. If a school is using the old traditional study halls, difficulties may result.

The following is a student's schedule:

Time	Monday	Tuesday	Wednesday	Thursday	Friday
8:00 9:45	A Chemistry	Individual Study	B Individual Study	A Chemistry	A Chemistry
	Guidance	Guidance	Guidance	Guidance	Guidance
10:00 11:45	C English	B Individual Study	C English	C English	B Individual Study
	L	U	N	C	H
12:25 2:10	E Physical Education	D Math	E Physical Education	D Math	D Math
2:15 4:00	F U.S. History	F U.S. History	Individual Study	F U.S. History	E Individual Study

STUDENT SCHEDULE

(105-minute module)

Holland High School, Holland, Michigan

The following is a teacher's schedule:

Time	Monday	Tuesday	Wednesday	Thursday	Friday
8:00 9:45	A U.S. History	Individual Conference	B World History	A U.S. History	A U.S. History
	Guidance	Guidance	Guidance	Guidance	Guidance
10:00 11:45	C Individual Conference	B World History	C Individual Conference	C Individual Conference	B World History
	L	U	N	C	H
12:25 2:10	E World History	D Individual Conference	E World History	D Individual Conference	D Individual Conference
2:15 4:00	F U.S. History	F U.S. History	Individual Conference	F U.S. History	E World History

HISTORY TEACHER SCHEDULE

(105-minute module)

Holland High School, Holland, Michigan

4. Broadly all other schedules are a combination of the previous three plans. Each school system will want to measure each of the ideas to determine the degree and amount of the innovations they wish to use. The following are other examples of schedules school administrators are using or planning to use:

Time	Monday	Tuesday	Wednesday	Thursday	Friday
8:00 9:55	U.S. History	Individual Conference	U.S. History	Individual Conference	U.S. History
10:00 11:55	World History	U.S. History	World History	U.S. History	World History
	L	U	N	C	H
1:00 2:55	World History	U.S. History	World History	U.S. History	World History

STUDENT SCHEDULE "A" WEEK
Clayton High School, Clayton, Missouri

Time	Monday	Tuesday	Wednesday	Thursday	Friday
8:00 9:55	Individual Conference	U.S. History	Individual Conference	U.S. History	Individual. Conference
10:00 11:55	U.S. History	World History	U.S. History	World History	U.S. History
	L	U	N	C	H
1:00 2:55	U.S. History	World History	U.S. History	World History	U.S. History

STUDENT SCHEDULE "B" WEEK
Clayton High School, Clayton, Missouri

Time	Monday	Tuesday	Wednesday	Thursday	Friday
8:00 9:55	Chemistry	Elective	Chemistry	Elective	Chemistry
10:00 11:55	English	Math	English	Math	English
	L	U	N	C	H
1:00 2:55	Physical Education	U.S. History	Physical Education	U.S. History	Physical Education

TEACHER SCHEDULE "A" WEEK
Clayton High School, Clayton, Missouri

Time	Monday	Tuesday	Wednesday	Thursday	Friday
8:00 9:55	Elective	Chemistry	Elective	Chemistry	Elective
10:00 11:55	Math	English	Math	English	Math
	L	U	N	C	H
1:00 2:55	U.S. History	Physical Education	U.S. History	Physical Education	U.S. History

TEACHER SCHEDULE "B" WEEK
Clayton High School, Clayton, Missouri

Time	Monday	Tuesday	Wednesday	Thursday	Friday
1					American History
2					
3	English II	Chemistry Lab.	English II	English II	
4					
	L	U	N	C	H
5	Algebra II	Activity	Chemistry Lecture	Chemistry Lecture	Activity
6		Physical Education	Algebra II	Chemistry Lab.	Physical Education
7	American History				
8			American History	Algebra II	

STUDENT SCHEDULE

(50-minute module)

Harbor Beach High School, Harbor Beach, Michigan

Time	Monday	Tuesday	Wednesday	Thursday	Friday
1	World History	Individual Conference	World History		American History
2				World History	
3	Government	Social Studies Team	Government		Team "A"
4				Government	Individual Conference
	L	U	N	C	H
5	Geography	Activity	Geography	Individual Conference	Activity
6		Geography			Geography
7	American History	Individual Conference	American History	Social Studies Team	Individual Conference
8					

SOCIAL STUDIES TEACHER SCHEDULE

(50-minute module)

Harbor Beach High School, Harbor Beach, Michigan

Time	Monday	Tuesday	Wednesday	Thursday	Friday
8:00	Chemistry	Elective	Chemistry	Elective	Chemistry
9:55					Elective
10:00	English	Math	English	Math	English
11:55					Math
	L	U	N	C	H
1:00	Physical Education	U.S. History	Physical Education	U.S. History	Physical Education
2:55					U.S. History

STUDENT SCHEDULE
Okemos High School, Okemos, Michigan

Time	Monday	Tuesday	Wednesday	Thursday	Friday
8:00	U.S. History	Individual Conference	U.S. History	Individual Conference	U.S. History
9:55					Individual Conference
10:00	U.S. History	World History	U.S. History	World History	U.S. History
11:55					World History
	L	U	N	C	H
1:00	World History	U.S. History	World History	U.S. History	World History
2:55					U.S. History

TEACHER SCHEDULE
Okemos High School, Okemos, Michigan

5. Most administrators have set a pattern for the schedule which is followed throughout the semester or year. At the present time some administrators are searching for ways to provide more flexible teach-

ing situations by changing the schedule throughout the school year.

The following is a description of this process:

Although students' schedules change daily according to teacher requests, it was recognized that students would have to have a daily base of operations from which to start their day. They were, accordingly, broken down into twenty groups of approximately twenty students per group. They divided the students according to elective choice, but any other method would work as well since the principal idea is to have the students identify with one stable group at the beginning of each day. Ninth grade teachers were assigned to the groups and became teacher-counselors for specific groups. Students report to the same teacher in the same room at the beginning of each school day to work out their schedules.

Students are identified by each instructional area team, according to their abilities and achievement levels, and assigned textbooks according to these ability groupings.

In planning the daily schedules, teachers meet with their Team Leaders to plot out the program in their instructional area. They determine the material to be covered, the groups they wish to meet, the time to be spent on each lesson, and the method of instruction desired—i.e., large-group instruction, small-group discussion, etc. This information is then recorded on a "Job Requisition" which each Team Leader takes to the Team Room to coordinate with the other Teams in setting up the Master Board. Requisition orders are set up on the board, conflicts are ironed out, rooms and teachers assigned, and the Master Schedule is ready to be transcribed and sent to each teacher-counselor for distribution to the students who will make out their daily program from this schedule.[1]

At this point you should lay out your own plan. Your attitude should change from one which sees why it cannot be done to one which sees the possibilities of this type of program. Experience has shown that, given a willing administrator with a willing staff backed by a patient and understanding school board, new and exciting schedules will be developed. Better education for all boys and girls can be the result. The challenge is open to every school staff in the country to do an even better job in bringing about instructional improvement.

CHAPTER 8

A Model: Independent Study in the Humanities

by

PHILLIP GEARHEART

Phillip Gearheart, a teacher of art and art methods for teachers, has worked with University School secondary students, with observers, and with teachers from the School of Education of Indiana University for five years. In addition to his work at the laboratory school, he has taught in the Fine Arts Department of the College of Arts and Sciences at Indiana University. Before joining the Indiana University faculty, he was on the staff at the University of Arkansas and the Park Forest Public Schools in Illinois.

INDEPENDENT STUDY is inquiry designed for exceptionally bright and creative students, pursued not as the student's total school experience but as enrichment or in place of regular classroom offerings which may not be challenging to the gifted student or in the absence of regularly scheduled accelerated programs. In these studies, the student is aided, not directed, in exploring, on his own, every facet of any problem which is of interest to him. He lets his intellectual curiosity carry him in any direction, crossing disciplines when necessary, and arrives perhaps at a point apparently far removed from the point of departure but in fact related to that point by the most valid connection of all, the searchings of his own curious mind.

This ending of a search is the ultimate satisfaction and the ultimate goal of study: learning for the joy of it. Independent study is best when it is individual. Content should not be bounded by a set program of studies. Gifted students are beyond that unfortunate educational preoccupation.

A Case Study

A sample of this type of study is given here in the record of a series of conferences which were held with a student of exceptionally high intelligence and talented in languages, music, and art. These conferences were held once a week with or without any actual physical creative products of the intervening week handed in, with discussion of thoughts and questions which had been raised by the work of the week, and with some decision reached about the direction of study for the next week.

FIRST CONFERENCE: With the line of inquiry suggested by the student's interest in the Russian language, the teacher and student talked about the contribution to music and literature made by Russia in the declining years of the nineteenth century and up until the revolution of 1917. It was decided to listen to Moussorgsky's opera *Boris Godunov* before the next meeting.

SECOND CONFERENCE: Listening to and reading about *Boris* produced a set of costume designs for the opera and led to discussion of The Five, the group of composers to which Moussorgsky belonged. This melted into a discussion of group action in the arts and to artistic manifestos in general. Some suggestions of materials were made. The artistry of Feodor Chaliapin, the most famous interpreter of the title role in *Boris,* was introduced and questioned.

THIRD CONFERENCE: The suprematist manifesto of 1916 led to interest in early twentieth-century art movements, with the discovery that Man Ray, a dadaist, was also a distinguished photographer. Thus, viewing some surrealist films next session was arranged.

FOURTH CONFERENCE: Teacher and student watched two surrealist films directed (and starred in) by Maya Deren. The word "Maya" triggered a discussion of pre-Columbian art and archaeology in general. For the next session it was decided to read *The Horizon Book of Lost Worlds, The Bull of Minos,* and *World of the Maya.*

FIFTH CONFERENCE: There had not been time to read all three, so the meeting was cancelled.

SIXTH THROUGH EIGHTEENTH CONFERENCE: The archaeological study suggested lost languages, so some time was spent discussing the initial decipherment of various dead languages. An interest in Minoan script and the island of Crete brought up the Minotaur Myth and all of Greek mythology. This lasted until longer than the semester and resulted in drawings illustrating myths, in some satirical writings in which modern myths were devised, and in experiments in etching motivated by Pablo Picasso's series of etchings, *Minotauromachia*.

The sketchy outline above cannot catalog the many tangential paths which were taken by the student in his inquiry, but it can indicate the tremendous breadth and depth of field which this sort of study can embrace. Each meeting of student and teacher was characterized by a great deal of give-and-take on the part of both. The teacher listened more than he talked in many sessions. Sometimes the questions raised by the student caused the teacher to become a student. Both student and teacher have work to do as the student's study develops.

Individuals in Independent Study

The fact that there are few American schools wherein the existing program leaves room for individual studies by exceptional youth bears testimony to the unfortunate inflexibility of current programs.[1] For administrative convenience, to meet accreditation's methodology of appraisal, to fit extant textbooks, out of inertia, in order to avoid the bother of changing the present setting of the automatic bell-ringing system, and for a host of other equally defensible reasons, nearly all American schools have set class periods, courses of study rigidly divided in an atomized way, and teacher specialists whose knowledge is more or less deep in a narrow subject area. To make individual study operative, a school needs to begin with assembling a community of scholars on the staff, do violence to the time-worn organization of the school day, and reread the requirements of the regional accrediting agencies. Students who do individual study need to be freed from group activity to pursue their diversified inquiry.

An adjunct of this inflexibility is regimentation. The corpus of education texts teems with hints and methods for inducing group consciousness in a student body. Today the teacher, faced generally with a mushrooming class size and the same number of desks as last year and the year before, is only too happy to be reassured that it is possible to get the mass of young humanity in step and safely away from the brink of an unknown area of study. In a very real sense it is necessary to be able partially to accomplish this aim, even if only to be able to find time to concentrate some attention on the creative students who can profit from individual study. However, the climate which has for generations been engendered by this rationale of regimentation is such that before the student can unbend to do individual study of a creative nature, both he and the teachers must devote considerable time to the task of unlearning years of anti-free orientation before any real progress can be made.

It would be comforting here to give a ten-step educational panacea to combat this lost feeling for freedom, but such is not realistic or compatible with the concept. It is likely that a high percentage of today's teachers will find it extremely difficult to come to know the internal freedom necessary to aid substantially the kind of learning which individual studies offer. Before individual studies can be made workable for today's teacher, there must be a period of adjustment wherein the old patterns of rigidity can be softened. A good example of freedom's confusing effect comes from the wail of students when told to write a paper on any topic or to do a drawing which expresses a sociological point of view. The immediate response is often one of bewilderment, and the secondary one is a plea for direction or for a rigid absolution from the necessity for choice. One can forcefully argue that this trait, which on gross examination would seem to be universally human, is learned and societal.

Experience with very young children, with students from experimental and permissive schools, and with exceptionally creative children has indicated that lack of flexibility in thinking and that sterile imagination is taught by inference, by example, and by practice in the school regimentations. How long has it been since even the school cafeteria offered a choice of lunches? Fear of failure and fear of a too radical departure from some artificial norm as well as sheer indecision caused by a faculty not used to having students making their own decisions all lead to convergent thinking and halt creativity.

To dispel the impression that this unfamiliarity with freedom is the only stumbling block placed before workable individual study, it must be mentioned that the administrative personality is not noted for a broad, laissez-faire world-view of instructional activity. As a matter of generic definition, the administrator covets and exists to impose order and, in the end, regimentation. For this reason, to convince the administrations that at least an attempt at individual studies is worthwhile is sometimes more difficult than to acquire a teacher who can handle the problems of teaching it. Until positive administrative leadership is shown in a school, individual independent study is nearly an impossibility.

Although the foregoing problems make difficult the implementation of individual studies, the final problem, the lamentable but not astonishing lack of preparation which hinders the average teacher, looms largest. One could never imply that teachers are not intelligent or that they are not hardworking. These would be unfair generalizations. However, it can be safely said that inadequate preparation in the liberal arts, the absurd demands to do trivial tasks which are made on the teacher's time by the housekeeping of the school, and a very human tendency to terminate intellectual growth after minimum competency has been attained are problems of teachers as a group.

Broad Fields Inquiry Problems

For example, inspect a sample student and a sample project in an integrated study in the liberal arts, and concurrently consider the training which the average teacher of English, for example, may have had which will help him aid the student in the search for knowledge.

The Project: an intensive study of the Impressionist movement in the arts.

The student: male, seventeen years old, I.Q. 145; insatiable curiosity.

The teacher: male, forty years old, I.Q. 117; curiosity somewhat dulled by sixteen years in the same old classroom.

Since our teacher majored in English and minored in social studies and, of course, education as an undergraduate, it is safe to assume

that he has taken some fifty to sixty-five semester hours of English
courses and an assortment of the required courses in other areas. As a
graduate, he took courses in both his academic area and professional
education. With this background, let us tabulate the avenues of inquiry which will be taken by the student and the relative ability of
the teacher to aid in them.

For a Start *Literature* Leads to

Impressionist poetry: The teacher will have had a three-hour
course in the poets of the second half of the nineteenth century
which will stand him in good stead.

which may lead to

Impressionist music: WHAT? says the teacher, blanching. Music
appreciation 101 didn't mention this. Here the teacher must go past
his formal education or a void in direction of the student is created.

which may lead to

Impressionist art: Here we are on firmer ground. Our teacher has a
print of a painting by Renoir, one of a little girl with a watering can,
which is wholesome and also the sum of our teacher's acquaintance with visual arts. (There was an option, music appreciation 101
or art appreciation 101. To select one was to neglect the other.)

which may lead to

Toulouse-Lautrec: This man is *not* so wholesome. How is he
presented? On the grounds of his unfortunate personal life, is his
contribution to art to be ignored? Did his life contribute to his
artistic production? Moral and ethical questions can be introduced
or ignored. There was little in the methods courses to cover these
questions. Can artistic license, which is supposedly acceptable, be a
pun?

which may lead to

Oscar Wilde: Lautrec did a devastating portrait of Wilde. What
about the preparation for handling these issues?

which may lead to

Social Problems: The social, artistic, and moral concerns of the
artist's versus society's mores. It may also lead back to the Impressionist poets or to the total breakdown of the project on the ground
that such subjects are not the proper concern of the class, and besides
the principal is extremely sensitive to such discussions, which lead

to community criticism! But what about the gifted scholar? Is he concerned with these matters?

In the tabulation, our student was not allowed to take nearly so many turns and tangents as he probably would have taken in actual practice, but the example is clear. With the inadequacy of background which is allowed, it is small wonder that few teachers are prepared to conduct individual studies of a high-level, interrelated nature.

Two simple but difficult to accomplish steps are necessary to correct this weakness. The first is to emphasize the interrelationship of fields. This is necessary at all levels of the educational system, not in college alone. The second is to somehow help teachers love learning for the sake of it. Give them an unquenchable thirst for knowledge. Provide the ability to be enthusiastic over a discovery, and to espouse the paraphrased view of Bacon: "All knowledge should be my province."

Conditions Set

In an attempt to talk about the positive side of this ephemeral business, some conditions are listed to aid in the implementation of this kind of learning and show how these conditions have been applied to specific situations.

CONDITIONS:

1. Careful selection of students and teachers for participation in the beginning, anyway, is required.
2. Complete trust of each for each must prevail.
3. Respect for privacy, the right to withhold products is helpful.
4. A most delicate balance of authority between teacher and student needs to be set.
5. Complete exploration of tangential questions must be encouraged.
6. Recognition of the difficulty of evaluation is essential.
7. Ability on the part of the teacher to handle problems resulting from students who become too involved with a problem or become unable to handle ramifications and implications of a concept must be recognized.

It is necessary to select only those students who have previously demonstrated a love of learning per se or who have suddenly and obviously acquired this condition for high-level individual study. Not only is time wasted on the unready or incapable student, but also the freedom and trust inherent in the implementation of this kind of study only serves to intensify dullness and to encourage intellectual delinquency and sloth where those traits already exist.[2]

The teacher who wishes to supervise individual studies by the method outlined above must be absolutely sure of his ability to grant the freedoms implied in the program and in his ability to keep up with the pace and agility of the student's mind. A teacher who finds himself lost halfway through one of these searches is as morally remiss as a brain surgeon who discovers, after opening the skull, that he does not really know what he is going to do. In essence, the teacher and student must be compatible, a rarely heard term in education where it is never considered important that there be genuine feeling between students and teacher. Again, this is an adjunct of mass-classes and anonymity. If this compatibility develops into a genuine rapport, then there is the possibility of communicating feelings which are impossible of verbalization. If already this description sounds akin to the relationship of psychiatrist to patient, it is purposefully so. A successful teacher by this method becomes so close to students that the role of supreme confidant and counselor is unavoidably added to the already heavy responsibilities involved. Before a teacher enters into a relationship with a student which may assume such great depth, he must be absolutely sure that he can handle the potentials of the situation.

Although trust extends into very personal matters in some cases, it must extend completely into the intellectual side of individual studies teaching. If there is doubt in the mind of the student that the teacher is insincere, bored, cynical, covering ignorance or otherwise not totally involved, the entire project can crumble. In addition, the teacher must allow the student to be unsupervised and often not available for lengthy questioning for long periods of time if the student so desires. Still the teacher must trust. I once allowed a student credit, if I may use the term here in the retail sense, on a project for an entire semester, issued an "A" each six weeks in compliance with the required efficiency on work as yet unseen and only briefly talked of. The completed study, an integrating of several disciplines, vindicated my trust but could have been depreciated had I insisted on prying. In other circumstances frequent checking and prodding is necessary.

The right of the creative person in every discipline to withhold his product until it is as complete and perfect as possible is inalienable. For those persons who value privacy, there is an element of intellectual peeping tom-ism inherent in overquestioning. It becomes stifling. Some brilliant students would destroy a partially completed work of art if it were to be peered at and criticized before completion. Such behavior may sound overly sensitive, in the tradition of the temperamental artist; but out of such feelings are truly creative products wrought. There is a stress involved in creation which is not describable but very real. Like certain poltergeists it exists on a mutually exclusive basis with insensitivity. Insensitive persons can never know it or see it and, thus, tend to disbelieve its existence.

Authority, Respect, and Freedom

In teaching of this kind there is only authority to the extent that there is respect. This balance of authority should be so delicate that there is no obvious exercise of it by either teacher or student. That respect is a function and a reflection of the intellectual stature and honesty of the participants. The least respected teachers attempt to gain respect by empty bombast and by the outward trappings of some professional authority. A highly starched shirt front is no substitute for a keen intellect. Daddyism has no place in any classroom for any student.

The freedom to explore all of the tangential questions which may occur is the feature of individual study which applies the maximum load to the teacher's knowledge. It is obvious that we cannot be a Socrates or a Renaissance polymath like Leonardo da Vinci. There will inevitably be areas of inquiry about which the teacher will be ignorant. However, if the teacher admits ignorance and immediately sets about becoming conversant with the area in question, then nothing is lost; and he has become a broader person with greater capabilities for the next problem. Even when a tangential avenue of inquiry is controversial and/or taboo, utterly bewildering in its scope or apparently trivial, it must be continued with until it has been exhausted or has led to another area of interest. One example of a development of the first type was a student who read *J.B.* This led to a study of the *Book of Job* and finally to a decision to compare all of the God-concepts in the history of man. This girl never finished but did some superior scholarship. Her reading was wide. Her written expression improved markedly. More important, her ability to handle divergent views was sharpened. Another student began with the study of hair styles. Little was found; little was learned. Little was gained. Contrary to the myth, all roads do not lead to Rome.

The unwillingness of most teachers to venture out of the protective shadow of their sphere of competency makes it likely that a teacher, perhaps of music, who is running individual study programs, will lead or channel the student into a circular path which is still in the general realm of music. This sort of behavior, although natural, contradicts the real spirit of individual study.

In every case the difficulty of evaluation arises because the only accurate judge of the benefits of study is the person who actually studied. Considering that professional measurement educators are prepared to admit the shallowness of evaluations arrived at by tests in the conventional subject-matter areas, how much more absurd it is to attempt to make evaluation in study which does not know the limits of an area. Letter grade evaluation, most always a subjective absurdity, becomes meaningless. If the student has produced an observable amount of concrete works, then it is possible to apply the old and inaccurate criteria of evaluation and arrive at a grade by the traditional method. However, if the student has only read deeply and learned to his satisfaction, how can he be assigned a letter commensurate with his gain? The solution (given the preceding conditions of selection, intelligence, etc.) is the student doing individual study is prima facie an "A" student, whatever "A" may mean. The sole merit of evaluation is in allowing the student to set forth clearly what he has come to know through a period of study. Also, it is a notice to parents that all is well. A teacher can never really know what a particular student actually knows except through telepathy.

Problems Arise

The problems which arise are, of course, as individual as the students who have them. In general, if this can be said, they follow two basic patterns:

A. The student becomes involved in one narrow path of inquiry to the exclusion of other alternatives, and often to the detriment of other school subjects.

This problem is not even a problem if we are to accept the prevalent view of specialization as the ultimate end of education. Neither is it a concern if we believe knowledge can be gained by an instructional mix. The study of literature involves far more than composition. All fields of the arts and sciences may be involved. Since most refuse to accept this view of education as a means of specialization, we try to manipulate discussion delicately so that other possibilities, more seductive perhaps, are introduced, and eventually the spell is broken. In any event, this temporary delay is not a catastrophe.

B. The student who intellectually, morally, or emotionally is unable to cope with the implications, ramifications, or scope of a concept. This is a more serious problem than the first one. If this situation develops, then the student should not have been studying individually at all. But of course this brilliantly hindsighted conclusion is of little help in solving the problem. The immediate solution is to cease individual study itself. This does not remove the problem from the student's mind but avoids any further fanning of the flames. Any long-term solution must come through professional psychiatrists, psychologists, or clergymen. An example of this failing was the extremely intelligent girl who, after a large number of excursions into literature extolling bohemianism, as a result of a devious train of interest going from stage design, to David Belasco, to *The Girl of the Golden West* by Puccini, to Puccini operas in general, to *La Bohème*, to Murger's *Scènes de la Vie de Bohème*, and to the beats of today, quit school entirely. It is this last danger which makes individual studies of the nature outlined suitable for only the most mature and gifted students. However, for those few it offers an unparalleled opportunity to discover the many dimensions of the liberal arts which are left unexplored by conventional school programs.

The Intelligent and the Creative

Individual studies stress the development of the creative trait which is in every individual. The degree to which the trait exists and can be personally developed varies. Experience has shown and research has verified the fact that intelligence and creativity are not necessarily companions with an individual.[3] Therefore, many intelligent students will do individual studies which lack originality and freshness. This does not fault their work but puts it in the context of their capability.

Experience seems to verify that the ability to think in new and original fashions can be increased or cultivated in all children. The end product has nearly as many variations as students. Much of the discussion in this chapter has been predicated on the belief that all gifted students should have the stimulation and opportunity to do original work. To arrive at new conclusions and to develop fresh beliefs are of benefit to all youngsters, regardless of their possession of creative capabilities. Thus individual study is for both the intelligent learner, regardless of the signs of creative ability, and the creative student.

In Retrospect

In this discussion the considerations have wandered from the reasons for individual study to the difficulties involved in implementing it. By considering the problems involved, light may be shed on changes which need to be made in order to make it possible for the schools to open the door to a widespread use of independent study.

The examples given are not prescriptive but descriptive. Formulas and predetermined tasks signify closed enterprises. The concern of independent study is open-ended inquiry. As has been noted, the role of the teacher is crucial and contrary to the schoolmaster connotations of early American teaching. Teachers become partners, often silent, in the satisfying and intriguing business of learning.

While other kinds or levels of independent study may exist, the concern here has been a program for the able and ambitious learner. Other chapters give reference to independent study for students of average or below average ability. Any of the several organizations for learning presented in Chapters Four, Six, or Seven will accommodate such a program as has been called for here.

CHAPTER 9

Technological Aids and Independent Study

by

JAMES L. OLIVERO

James L. Olivero, principal of Poway High School in California, received his doctor's degree from Stanford University. He has visited over 170 schools as a consultant, speaker, and supervisor of interns. Before going to Stanford, James Olivero was an administrator at Lakeview High School, Decatur, Illinois, during the time the De-catur-Lakeview Plan was inaugurated. He is one of the authors of Team Teaching: Bold New Venture.

ANY INSTRUCTIONAL PROGRAM designed to individualize learning should not overlook the important role which can be played by the multimedia aids. In the context of this chapter multimedia aids are defined as those materials which elicit multisensory (e.g., sight, smell, touch, etc.) responses from the student. Certainly, educational psychologists have confirmed the theory that instruction via the multimedia aids can produce modifications of behavior through learning. The concept of multimedia aids suggests a predetermined rate and mode of presentation without continued direction by the teacher. (Hereafter, the symbol "MMA" will represent "multimedia aids.")

Examples of MMA are: tape recorders, records, mock-ups, filmstrips, still and moving pictures, mock-downs, television, maps, globes, programmed learning materials, reading accelerators, microprojectors, and so forth. The list could go on and on *ad infinitum,* but examples of the MMA are inappropriate unless the teacher can use

141

the aids as additional tools for improving the quality of instruction generally and individualizing the instruction specifically.

The Multimedia: Their Value in Individualized Instruction

Perhaps, some teachers associate the MMA with mass audiences; certainly, the MMA are more frequently used in the traditional school with mass audiences and demonstration techniques than with independent study. Delimiting the scope of the role demanded for the MMA, however, limits the effectiveness of the tools. Practically, MMA can be used effectively not only for mass audiences but also for individuals. If the multimedia are able to provide information and understanding for mass audiences, they should also be able to provide motivation and background knowledge for most individuals. The main question, then, that teachers and administrators must answer is: "What role can the MMA fulfill in the school's attempt to individualize instruction?"

Certainly, the teacher and administrator cannot consider the MMA and their influence apart from the totality of the learning experiences provided by the schools. The MMA must be considered as a part of the regular teaching and learning program. Whatever contributions the MMA can provide must be consistent with the general goals and objectives of the school. For example, the following diagram might well represent a skeletal outline of the school's concern for the learning activities of the students.

CONSIDERATION OF STUDENT LEARNING ACTIVITIES

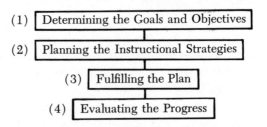

(1) ☐ Determining the Goals and Objectives

(2) ☐ Planning the Instructional Strategies

(3) ☐ Fulfilling the Plan

(4) ☐ Evaluating the Progress

(1) The first step any staff must take, as far as specific learning activities are concerned, is to determine the goals and objectives the school seeks to accomplish. (2) The staff must then plan instructional

strategies to achieve the goals. To complete the learning sequence the teachers must (3) attempt the strategies and (4) assess the effectiveness of the various strategies. At step two of this four-step process the staff must consider using MMA. After the goals have been determined, the members of the staff need to determine what resources are available to accomplish the goals. If multimedia aids can help students achieve goals, the aids should be employed.

Alert staffs are aware of most of the resources at their command. There is a need, however, for individuals in the schools to define clearly the role which the MMA can play as a means for individualizing the instruction. The school faculty must not only be cognizant of the available resources, but the faculty must also seek to implement the resources effectively. Each school, obviously, has certain resources available. The effective teacher is cognizant of these resources and plans his instructional strategies so both he and his students can take full advantage of them. Although the MMA equipment encompasses only one portion of the total resources of the school, administrators and teachers need to seek more appropriate methods for utilizing existing resources, resources available to generate a greater output. In the diagram, "input" represents the existing MMA. The "utilization of equipment" box in the diagram represents the use made of the equipment. The utilization of equipment depends upon the imagination and creativeness of the members of the school staff and what the school staff understands about the available resources on the one hand and the attainment of goals on the other. The greater the effective utilization (emphasis being on the word "effective"), the greater the output. It is possible, therefore, for two schools to have exactly the same resources, but one school may have a greater output if it can utilize the available MMA to a substantially greater degree.

There is no question that teachers must make better instructional use of their resources. Pertinent probing questions might include the following: "How many filmstrips are used only once or twice each year?" "What use can be made of the maps which are stored in the library?" These questions are examples of those which should be asked by staff members interested in surveying the available MMA. Clearly, complete utilization of resources is not being realized in most schools. However, schools must take advantage of every opportunity to provide students with worthwhile learning experiences; the MMA can share in this responsibility. If the teacher adopts the attitude that the MMA should wear out from overuse, as opposed to old age, he will approach a realistic understanding of the multitude of opportunities which await the student in his search for knowledge.

The MMA are not implemented into the instructional program to eliminate the teacher. (If a teacher can be replaced by a machine, he probably needs to be replaced.) It is possible, though, that the role of the teacher may be somewhat altered. As opposed to his traditional role as disseminator of knowledge, the teacher who makes wise use of the MMA acts as an informed guide, assisting students to explore a variety of sources for answers to the student's pressing questions. What teacher can compete with most commercially prepared materials, materials developed through the combined efforts of many professionally competent individuals?

Teachers undoubtedly can and do compete; however, to synthesize all of the necessary material for meeting individual student needs, the teacher obviously needs to spend many hours preparing relatively small samples of learning materials. The costs in terms of teacher time, energy, and effort may be too great for the rewards. When costs exceed rewards, the teacher must consider other alternatives. Rather than preparing the material himself, the teacher may elect to refer the right student to the right prepared materials. By following this procedure the teacher has not averted his responsibility; but indeed, he has utilized additional resources to meet at least two objectives: (1) increased subject-concentration for the student, and (2) decreased time-commitment for the teacher. Only experience and continued experimentation will determine how technological tools can best be used to generate increased student achievement.

Many schools are using a variety of MMA to provide individualized instruction. The remainder of the chapter will be devoted to some thoughts about the kinds of learning activities which can realistically be recognized via the MMA. In addition, some general guides for gaining maximum utilization from existing resources will be discussed.

Tapes

Probably the least expensive, but potentially one of the most powerful multimedia tools, is the magnetic tape. In most schools tapes have found their way into the language laboratory, but little use is made of tapes in most other disciplines. Even in foreign language classes, the full potential of tape usage is seldom realized. In addition to their usual function, that is, drill exercises, audio-feedback, etc., it is possible for some schools to offer an elective foreign language, a language not ordinarily offered in the regular school curriculum, by using tapes. Students can study the tapes during independent study. With today's emphasis on the conversational approach to foreign languages, tapes that have been prepared by individuals who use the correct intonation and pronunciation may help students more than a teacher who has had minimum preparation in the alternative foreign language. Whatever the case, independent study by foreign language students using tapes is not only educationally sound, but technically feasible.

The language laboratory can also be used to provide additional independent study by tapes for students in foreign languages. Most language laboratories are equipped with multiple, master-tape decks. It is possible, therefore, to use more than one tape deck at any given time. One teacher, working with a regularly assigned class in the laboratory, can easily turn the switches on another tape deck and thereby, with a minimum of effort, assist students in a different language as the students study independently. Some schools have as many as three different groups of students working on independent study in a language laboratory while another class works with a teacher in an assigned class. This type of independent study works equally well with tape or cartridge laboratories; however, there is slightly less teacher-time required for cartridge type laboratories than for the regular type laboratories.

Language laboratories are relatively expensive and most administrators attempt to schedule the laboratories for complete utilization. Language laboratories that remain idle for days at a time not only are financially unsound but also are educationally unjustified. Tapes can be used for independent study in the language laboratory for purposes other than foreign language training. For instance, students in speech classes can make good use of tapes in the language laboratory. The students can listen to assigned speeches which have been put on tapes, or they can practice dictation exercises which the teacher has assigned. Students, like teachers, seldom have the opportunity to hear themselves as others hear them. The students can make responses to the tapes and then listen to their responses until desired mastery is attained. Also, speech and drama students can critique themselves during independent study by listening to tapes made of their class presentations.

Business classes can also effectively use the language laboratory during independent study. Some schools have found that dictation tapes can be played for shorthand students in independent study, and the students can gain excellent experience by listening to the tapes and practicing their shorthand skill. The language laboratory with the multiple tape decks enables students to work at their own pace. For example, if one student has gained greater speed-skill than another student, he can work with a tape that has been recorded at a faster word-pace.

There are countless possibilities for which tapes and the language laboratory can be used by students during independent study. Experimentation and imaginative innovation have doubtlessly produced other sound, independent study activities which have not been outlined in the aforementioned paragraphs. Much remains to be explored.

The language laboratory is not the only place where independent study by tape can take place. Anything that can be accomplished by tapes in a language laboratory can also be accomplished using a tape recorder in a study carrel or in any other appropriate soundproof area. Headphones attached to the tape recorder even eliminate the need for a soundproof listening space.

Tapes are used by students for independent study in many disciplines. Recognizing individual need for spelling improvement, English teachers have prerecorded spelling words on tapes and have had students practice spelling drills during independent study. The student listens to the teacher as the teacher pronounces and slowly spells the words. Following the teacher's directions, the student practices spelling the words. Students who have participated in independent study such as the one described have shown marked improvement in a needed skill area.

Knowing that a particularly important speech will be given during the school day, some schools have made arrangements with ladies from the P.T.A. or other helpful people in the community to tape record broadcasts or other important presentations. Students can listen and analyze the content on the tapes during independent study if the teacher elects not to replay the tape for the entire class. Some tapes are appropriate for all individuals while other tapes may be appropriate for specific students who have definite interests and/or needs.

Music teachers have used tapes very advantageously by having students in independent study listen to outstanding works of music, both for pleasure and for understanding. Instrumental instructors have asked students to record on tape samples of the music exercises practiced during independent study learning sessions. By playing back the tapes students are able to identify those passages which cause them tone or articulation difficulties, and the students are then able to attack specific, identifiable problems. The feedback the students receive from the tapes tells them how well they are doing, and they can redirect their learning experiences accordingly. The tape can also serve as a training record for the teacher who is not present during the independent study activity.

Also a business department project can use tapes for independent study. Some stenography students enrolled in advanced business courses have gained valuable experience from assimilated training activities practiced during independent study. Students listen to tapes which provide directions for the students to follow; the tapes help the student simulate an actual job-situation. The tapes often include such things as telephone calls, letters which are dictated and need to be transcribed, and specific directions for filing. A complete work-experience can be practiced by the student in an independent study session. The student is able to analyze his mistakes and to take necessary corrective action. When the student passes one tape with accepted proficiency, he is able to attempt more difficult and complex learning experiences on other tapes.

Independent study using tapes can be exciting and challenging for students as well as demanding for teachers. Most teachers welcome the opportunity to use their creative abilities to explore untraveled avenues that may lead to worthwhile learning experiences for students.

Disk Recordings (Records)

Anything that can be accomplished by recording tapes can also be accomplished by disk recordings, more commonly called records. The specific independent learning activities outlined in the section on magnetic tapes can be adapted to fit the limitations of disk recordings. Generally speaking, recordings on disks may have a longer life expectancy than recordings on tapes; for this reason, some schools have employed disks to a greater degree than recording tapes. Tapes may have other advantages; however, this discussion is not for the purpose of comparing the alternative media, but rather to make the point that independent study activities, which demand sound playback, can be obtained from disk as well as magnetic recordings.

In addition to the independent study activities mentioned in the previous section, many teachers have planned additional enriched learning activities for children by using disk recordings. For example, disks have the very practical advantage that they can be played on the record players in many of the students' homes. Thus, independent study need not be confined to the four walls of the school. If a social studies teacher decides that a specific student in his class should listen and respond to former President Dwight D. Eisenhower's farewell address, the teacher can use the prepared records to re-create the tenseness and drama provoked at the original historical event.

English teachers have often used materials on records to stimulate students in independent study. Students, individually or in small groups of four or five, have listened to recordings of talented artists present readings from Frost and Sandburg; or the students have listened attentively and enthusiastically to *Hamlet* or *Julius Caesar*. Frequently and usually productively the listening activities made possible by disk recordings expand upon the specific learning activities highlighted in the classroom.

Some typing teachers have developed records which their students use during independent study. On records drill exercises designed to facilitate finger dexterity have been both popular and helpful for beginning typists. Students learning the keyboard need much drill work and some students more than others. Typing students in independent study can play the appropriate record and follow the directions of the teacher as the voice commands, "d-f, d-f, m-n, m-n, etc." The student who needs additional practice can work as long as necessary, while the student who demonstrates criteria mastery is able to move ahead to a more difficult assignment. Schools that have attempted this independent study project have found that some students need not remain in a typing class for an entire semester; indeed, when the student demonstrates the required course competencies, he is free to work in another curricular area of his interest. The student is rewarded for his achievement, and the teacher's class size is reduced to the point that it is possible for the teacher to spend additional time with students who need the extra assistance.

Physical education teachers, particularly the women, have used records for independent study more extensively, perhaps, than most other teachers. Students using records have been engaged productively in physical exercises, modern dances, and rhythm studies. The student can work by himself or with a few other students as he listens and responds to the audio stimulus. Students accept and appreciate the opportunity to demonstrate their creative and imaginative responses to the records.

Obviously, the foreign languages and the music teachers can also use disk recordings quite well to augment their curricular offerings via independent study. Other teachers, given time to brainstorm, will be able to determine specific innovations using disk recordings for their subject areas.

Models (Mock-Ups and Mock-Downs)

Students have found that models, mock-ups and mock-downs, are frequently better aids for study than the actual item. For example, students studying independently in biology are able to handle and examine model replicas of the internal organs in a human body. Certainly, it would be far too impractical to provide students with the real thing. Students taking courses in the biological and physical sciences use models frequently, generally of the mock-up variety. They are models which are larger in actual size than the real thing.

Mock-downs are often used by students taking courses in the industrial arts. If students are studying the complex operation of an automobile's transmission, the students may find that a needed transmission is not available. Moreover, there may be a real transmission handy but the students may be able to learn more efficiently and effectively by utilizing the model. Some industrial arts teachers have had their students practice with models of a transmission during independent study times so the students can build up or break down the transmission with little or no hesitancy about the necessary steps that must be taken.

Globes and maps are included in the MMA under the general heading of "Models." A resource center with maps and globes available for student use helps to provide additional tools for study learning activities.

Driver training students can take advantage of models by using miniature automobiles and highways to simulate actual conditions. The decisions a student makes about his driving responsibilities during independent study practice sessions will carry over to his behind-the-wheel performance. One complicated model that has been used for driver's training of students is the Drivotrainer. This model is a full-scale reproduction of a driver's station behind a wheel. Students who progress slowly in mastery of competency in their behind-the-wheel training can spend many valuable hours practicing in the Drivotrainer.

Models are particularly appropriate when the real things cannot be brought to the school environment because of the expense of the item, because of the scarcity of the item, or because of the danger of the item. Teachers of social studies, physical and biological sciences, industrial arts, homemaking, and driver education have been particularly perceptive in their understanding about the role for models in independent study activities. Clearly, many additional examples of effective use for models might be given. Any good audiovisual source book suggests numerous possibilities. However, the implementation of ideas into an operational procedure is more easily stated than accomplished.

Slides and Filmstrips

Slides and filmstrips are both dealt with in this section because they usually use the same projector to produce their pictures. However, slides and filmstrips may serve different purposes for independent study programs. Filmstrips generally focus on a central issue; also, the frames in a filmstrip are arranged in a sequential pattern, providing emphasis and continuity. Slides generally carry a one-picture message; they are, perhaps, more flexible than specific filmstrips.

Art teachers have found that the flexibility of slides can help bring many of the world's great art treasures into the student's limited environment. On independent study the student can move from one slide to another as quickly or as slowly as he desires. The student may want to practice sketch works from the masters' paintings during the student's concentration and depth training period.

With today's fast travel and the reduced time-space between the continents, many students and teachers who have traveled widely have added historical and documentary slides to the school's collection. The English and social studies teachers can take advantage of these materials by helping students be aware of the offerings the slides provide. Students with special interests and backgrounds can wisely utilize some of their independent study time by taking advantage of the available slide materials.

Students of mathematics, particularly geometry students, are able to analyze slides of bridges and other architectural structures for practical application of geometric principles. In many cases it is impossible or impractical to take the students to the structures, but it is possible and practical with slides to bring the structures to the students. Slides can be used by students on individual study either as a follow-up to material presented by teachers in large-group presentations or as explorations in depth, expanding upon student interests about various mathematical principles.

Advanced mechanical drawing students may be able to use their independent study time to advantage by reviewing slides which depict, for example, outstanding construction accomplishments. Students with mechanical drawing skill can examine slides of Frank Lloyd Wright creations and, perhaps, gain individual insight into the solution of their own problems. Two or three students frequently work together on this type of individual study to synthesize mixed perceptions about those things they observe.

Although filmstrips may be less flexible than individual slides, filmstrips have an important function for individual and independent study. Filmstrips usually provide accurate and up-to-date information about relatively limited material. Moreover, commercially prepared filmstrips usually have accompanying study guides that are very helpful to the student. Study guides provide additional supplementary material. Filmstrips are frequently used in large group presentations; students who have difficulty grasping the one-time presentation can review the filmstrips during independent study time and recapitulate the main ideas and concepts. Commercially prepared filmstrips can provide enriched resource information, and in this regard they are very appropriate for individual activities.

Art students have used the sequential organization pattern of filmstrips to learn about the steps followed for silk screen productions. In addition, the students have used filmstrips to increase their knowledge by surveying a particular period in art, a particular artist's works, or a particular style of art.

Business teachers have had their students study filmstrips for specific answers to a variety of specific problems. For example, a student who is having difficulty in an accounting or bookkeeping class can improve his competency by reviewing a filmstrip that outlines the step-by-step entry procedures for cost accounting. The student can spend as much time as necessary comparing his own problems and entries with the explanations and entries he sees on the filmstrip projections. This type of independent study activity is particularly rewarding to the student because he is able to think through the answers to his own problems. If one objective for the school and the course is to help students think, students must be given the opportunity and the freedom to seek correct answers.

Filmstrips are used quite advantageously by students in foreign language courses. The students are able to gain a deep appreciation for the culture of the country whose language is being learned. Most foreign language teachers complain that they rarely have time to teach about the country because they must spend each minute in class reviewing and reinforcing the students' vocabulary. Filmstrips offer excellent opportunities for students to study independently and to gain desired cultural appreciation.

There are an infinite number of filmstrips which have application for independent study in English, social studies, and the physical and biological sciences. Students can use the abundant filmstrip resources for either enriched or remedial study, depending upon the specific individual needs. One of the reasons individualized instruction by filmstrip is held in high regard for slow learners, or other students who have learning difficulties in a specific phase of a course, is the removal of extraneous factors (other students, perhaps) which have the tendency to distract the learner from the teacher's predetermined goals.

Although filmstrips are available for almost every major subject and some relatively minor topics, complete advantage of this medium has not been recognized. Most schools and/or school districts have catalogs which list titles and give annotations about specific filmstrips for use in almost all subject areas. One of the major concerns for most administrators and staff members is the availability of funds for filmstrips and slide projectors. When one considers the life-expectancy and use-ratio of filmstrips, the $25 expenditure becomes insignificant. Most schools which use filmstrips extensively for independent study have ruled against the regular filmstrip projector. Instead, they have adopted inexpensive ($2.50) individual viewers. The viewers accommodate slides as well as filmstrips. An inexpensive projector, coupled with effective but inexpensive filmstrips and slides, can provide students with educationally well-produced materials— materials necessary for tapping the individual learning potential for all children. Slides and filmstrips are additional resources schools must utilize if they are to increase the value of their output.

Television

Few students in even fewer schools throughout the country receive any of the potential benefits afforded by open- or closed-circuit television. And although television is most frequently associated with mass audiences, television need not be limited strictly to mass audiences. Open-circuit television includes both commercial and educational television offerings while closed-circuit TV is basically limited to a school or school district. Commercial television frequently has programs which offer documentary and challenging information for individual students. Educational television stations often have special courses, as well as programs of special interest, which are offered during the school day. Closed-circuit programs can be tailored to meet the specific needs and interests of the students.

Unfortunately, many schools that operate on a traditional schedule have difficulty coordinating open-circuit programs with the restrictions inherent in the traditional lockstep schedule. Other schools that have adopted schedules which are formed from modular building blocks of twenty to thirty minutes are flexible enough to permit individual or small groups to review specific programs. Schools with the occupationally hazardous restrictions of small enrollments and limited funds are frequently prohibited from offering courses for which there is little demand. These courses, trigonometry, calculus, and so forth, are important; and these schools may be able to offer the advanced courses from instruction via open-circuit television, particularly from the educational television channels.

Programs on commercial stations often present topics that are particularly appropriate for English and social studies students. In addition to the drama productions, the panel discussions about current events and the documentary programs seem to hold most promise for individualized instruction. The programs are usually well-produced and are stimulating for most academically oriented students. In addition to the many English and social studies topics, there are a number of programs which portray the role of science and technology in our changing, urban-industrial society.

Although only a handful of schools are using closed-circuit television, the recent invention of the portable video television recorder will undoubtedly open many avenues for improved instruction— mass as well as individualized. Ampex and Precision Optical have developed a lightweight and relatively inexpensive video recorder which promises to be used in many schools, particularly those schools in which the administrators and teachers exert their creative and imaginative influences. The audiovisual recorders use one-inch magnetic tapes which can be erased and used over and over. The video recorder seems to have particular application for students who are developing individual skills. If a school has its own television recorder, the school may be able to purchase or to produce tapes which can be used by students who have requested courses that the school is unable to offer.

Video tapes can be used by speech and drama students during independent study. For example, speech and drama students can make a presentation and then listen and watch themselves. Some teachers insist that the best students in speech courses are those who can constructively criticize their own efforts. If the teachers are correct, individual students who are able to watch themselves on the television monitor should be able to improve more than students who receive only verbal feedback from teachers and other students.

Few schools take advantage of the educationally important community resources. By using the portable video recorder where it has been impossible for the students to visit the source, some schools have been able to bring the source to the students. A theatrical production, an art exhibit, a political campaign speech, and so forth, can all be brought to the students by video recordings. The experiences described may be applicable for large groups of students; however, if the teacher elects not to use the recorded material, individual students should not be denied the opportunity to use what is available.

It was mentioned earlier that skills can be taught easily by using the video recordings. Students learning skills in physical education programs, skills such as shooting a basketball, doing stunts on the parallel bars, and diving from a highboard are usually able to make rapid improvement after they have been able to observe themselves on the video recordings and after they have been able to analyze their mistakes. The immediate feedback which the video tape provides seems to eliminate incorrect performances which sometimes become engraved when the participant has no knowledge of how well he has performed his specialty.

Video recordings have also been used effectively for science demonstrations. Some demonstrations are very difficult to see when viewed from the rear of a large lecture room. However, video tape can usually record the dissection of a frog or other experiments by making use of a close-up or zoom lens; then the viewer is able to see all of the intricate operations performed by the instructor. If the student is unclear about the procedures followed during the major presentation, he can review the video tapes for additional clarification during his independent study time.

Video tapes can be used to record large-group presentations; thus students who have been absent from school on the days the original lectures are given can use their independent study time and the tapes to catch up on the work they have missed. Obviously, there are very few schools than can sacrifice a $12,000 piece of equipment to the untrained fingers of most students (and teachers?). The video equipment is flexible enough to permit the recorder to be placed in one location under the watchful eyes of a trained technician who places the desired tape on the playback reel while at the same time a student can watch a monitor that has been placed in another location. Then the student in individual study merely is required to turn the "on—off" switch on the table monitor. Certainly, anything which can be heard or seen can be recorded on video tapes to produce the desired instructional and informational programs.

Some research has indicated that students taught by television score significantly higher on tests than students taught in the conventional manner, particularly when the subject matter was concerned with small parts of a major topic. The myriad uses of television for independent study may provide the long overdue impetus for improved teaching techniques, while at the same time facilitating individualized learning.

Programmed Learning

It is the purpose of this discussion neither to assess the relative merits of linear or branching programs nor to comment upon the differences in learning rates between students who study from programmed texts and students who study from teaching machines. Clearly, educational literature is replete with research studies which substantiate the claim that students can and do show significant learning improvement after they have completed various programmed learning materials. Suffice it here to say that the learning improvement which any student makes is dependent upon the quality of the program and the active involvement in the learning process by the student.

Programmed materials are auto-instructional devices designed in such a way that the program content helps a student move from the known to the unknown in a step-by-step progression. Programs are tied together by a series of frames which generally include at least three components—a predetermined response, a setting or context from which the response is to be elicited, and specific and relevant cues which are emphasized in such a way that they will stimulate the desired response. Many programs deviate from this central theme by adding additional enrichment statements or review statements; however, all of the programs include the three basic elements.

Programmed instruction is relatively new and, therefore, suffers from a lack of empirical evidence. Most of the evidence comes from controlled experiments conducted by educational psychologists. A few school districts, such as the Roanoke district in Virginia and the Pittsburgh Public School District, have made extensive studies to determine the effectiveness of programmed materials. Both experiments were highly successful in terms of improved learning for the participants.

Auto-instructional programs for independent study are rapidly being produced. There are complete instructional programs in areas such as economics, statistics, algebra, geometry, English grammar, poetry, flag etiquette, and the foreign languages.

Examples of the wide range of categories included within the ever expanding confines of programmed instruction were clearly indicated at a facetious award ceremony held at the University of California. Awards were made for the following programs:

> *Largest Program in Actual Feet:* H. O. Holt, Bell Telephone Labs, "Basic Electricity" (2225 feet).
> *Highest Sheer Bulk:* A. A. Lumsdaine and David Klaus, American Institute for Research, "High School Physics" (approximately three large telephone books, 3000 items).
> *Most Impossible Subject Matter:* Robert Gogne, Princeton, "Quinary Numbers" and Evan Keislar, UCLA, "Molecular Theory for First Grades."
> *Having Courage Where Commercial Giants Fear to Tread:* Lloyd Homme, Teaching Machines, Inc. (Seven commercially available programs—Statistics, Russian, Music, etc.).
> *Showing Psychologists How to Use the Printed Page:* Harcourt Brace, "English 2600," programmed text of 2600 items on 440 small, attractive pages.[1]

Programmed learning material is applicable at both ends of the student learning continuum. Programmed material can be used as enrichment materials for students who want to go above and beyond minimum course requirements, or the programmed materials can be used for remedial teaching purposes. Inherent in auto-instructional materials is a content format which enables students to progress according to their own rate of learning. Programmed materials are also very practical for small schools, if the schools are interested in providing learning experiences in subjects normally not offered in the regular school curriculum.

Programmed material is relatively inexpensive. Most programs now come in well-arranged kits which permit easy student access but also prohibit destruction, other than the normal wear and tear. A single programmed text can be used by four or five students who check the text in and out of the instructional materials center during their independent study time.

Teachers have had some success producing programmed materials for their courses, particularly materials which deal with processes or procedures that are generally difficult to teach in a lecture-discussion approach. Unfortunately, most teachers do not have the time necessary to write, test, and rewrite a program which can be used by most students. When teachers do have time, or when they make time, they frequently find that the experience of writing a program helps them to think through their own specialty more carefully. In this case, the programmed materials are rewarding for the teachers as well as for the students.

Even though there are a variety of programs available, mathematics programs seem to be favorites for high school students taking advantage of independent study opportunities. Programs for English and spelling, written by authors who have used a variety of approaches, are also available. It is up to the educational astronauts in our schools, those teachers and administrators who are always a little out in space in terms of the different innovations they use to improve the quality of instruction, to use and to assess the value of programmed materials for meeting the objectives of the schools. Auto-instructional devices hold untested advantages for students engaged in independent study. The gap between the psychological learning principles built into the programmed materials and the practical application of the principles in the classroom is being significantly reduced. Perhaps time will help to bridge the gap completely.

Motion Pictures

Not too many years ago, the use of motion pictures for independent study would have been impractical. Today, with the improvements that have been made in the various 8 mm. and 16 mm. projectors, the use of moving pictures becomes an added tool for student use. For example, the complicated threading procedures, which are typical for some types of projectors, have been replaced by self-threading projectors. The viewer merely places the reel in the spindle, turns the button to "on," and the machine does the rest. Not only does this eliminate many of the traumatic experiences which have confronted teachers for many years, but also this type of projector reduced the amount of wear and tear on the film.

The self-threading movie projector seems to be the only practical projector for student use in independent study. These projectors will accommodate both 16 mm. and 8 mm. films. This type of projector is recommended because most students do not know how to thread a projector; and unfortunately, when students have difficulties, the life-expectancy of the films is substantially reduced. In schools that have only the conventional type projector, student projectionists can be trained to run films for other students during independent study.

Another recent moving picture projection innovation includes the manufacture of relatively inexpensive cartridge reels that run from two to five minutes. These cartridges use projectors that take very little space. The miniature projectors can be used quite easily in study carrels or in any other place where there is an outlet. The student simply slides the cartridge into the projector and the self-winding cartridge completes its regular topic-cycle.

A number of cartridges have been developed for students who have special interests in biology. For instance, one two-minute cartridge very clearly portrays the process of mitosis. Because the cartridge is self-winding, the student can replay the filmclip as often as desirable.

The cartridge type projectors are also very practical for physical education students who work during independent study time to improve their skills. For example, if a student is interested in learning how to serve a volleyball, he may be able to review a two-minute cartridge presentation and then practice the serve. Other skills are also included in the cartridge series, including tumbling, handball, and weight lifting. Clearly, the technological assistance gained from the films may help a student already practicing a given skill to improve his abilities even further by providing a model on the film which the student can imitate.

Cartridges are presently being produced for most of the NDEA subject-sponsored areas: science, mathematics, and the foreign languages. All of the cartridge materials can be used by students in independent study.

Research has indicated that films can be used as the sole means for teaching some kinds of factual material; certainly for performance skills and factual information, films can be important tools. Most districts, school or county, have printed lists which indicate the number and kinds of films available. If teachers have previewed films, they can often add substance to the student's viewing by developing guide-points which the students should use as they view the film. In addition, guide questions may also be developed; the questions are answered by the student after he has seen the film. Some schools have used this type of activity to develop student-teacher leadership skills. That is, after one student has previewed a film, he makes guide points and questions for other students to use at subsequent showings.

In addition to the regular individual study assignments which are made in all of the subject areas, some schools have used films as part of their cultural enrichment program. The cultural enrichment programs are designed to help young people who come from culturally disadvantaged homes to see by film many of the sights they undoubtedly would never see in their life experiences. This use of the film materials is very rewarding for these students.

Students are beginning to use films during the independent study time to provide a different perspective about a particular project on which the students are working. For instance, if a student were writing a research paper about the Elizabethan era, in addition to the material he might find in book sources, he may also be able to use some films to gain additional information or different interpretations about his topic. Thus the films become an additional source tool which is available to the student.

The use of films for independent study usually requires definite planning on the part of the teacher and the student. The rewards derived from an activity of this nature far exceed the costs if the required planning reduces the administrative snags and if the film significantly improves the quality of instruction for the student.

Reading Accelerators

One technological device that is particularly applicable for independent study is the reading accelerator. This automatic projector uses filmstrip-type materials as its visual medium. The projector can be regulated to flash the filmstrip material on the screen at any given speed, from a reading speed of very few words-per-minute to a reading speed of approximately 1,000 words-per-minute. The student can vary the speed of the tachistoscope-type projector according to his own needs. If a student reads slowly and he would like to read more rapidly, he adjusts the pacer so the sentences are flashed onto the screen at a relatively faster rate. As the student's competence improves, he can increase the projector's pacing. Perhaps another student may be interested in developing greater speed and comprehension for specialized material. By practicing during his independent study time, the student is able to determine his optimum speedpace for quality comprehension. Although there is conflicting research about the values of the tachistoscope reading projectors for all students, there seems to be substantial evidence that the flash materials work very well for some students. Teachers need to work closely with students to determine the applicability of the equipment for the desired goals.

The reading accelerator can be used appropriately for other independent study activities. For instance, typewriting students have used the equipment to flash sentences on the screen. The typing student reads the sentence and types out the information. As the student's typing ability improves, the flash-pace is increased. This activity has stimulated some otherwise average typists to meet the "A" criteria.

When words are used rather than sentences, the flash projections can be utilized to develop spelling competency. This type of projection may make little use of the phonic approach to spelling, but for some students the technique seems to be effective.

Some mathematics teachers have used the tachistoscope as an aid for students. The tachistoscope concept can be adopted for independent study in mathematics to increase number recognition speed and to increase the recognition span.

The reading accelerator can be a valuable tool for independent study.

Technological Tools

By no means have all of the audiovisual tools been mentioned and certainly even fewer of the potential learning activities. In addition to the equipment mentioned, micro-projectors, lantern-slide projectors, still cameras, and so forth might have been included in the aforementioned discussion. A recent experiment in San Diego County tested one hundred sixty-seven different pieces of audiovisual equipment for independent study use. Probably no school possesses the financial resources to provide one hundred sixty-seven different MMA; moreover, quantity is far from the most important consideration. However, the point is that there are pieces of equipment which will meet almost every conceivable individual need.

The MMA tools are only important when and if they can help students meet their needs. Therefore, teachers need to consider what goals are desirable and what resources are available to meet the goals. If the inherent potentials of the MMA can be helpful for students to meet goals, the MMA must be used. The myriad potential uses of the MMA are relatively untried; this fertile field must be cultivated. As teachers have time during the school day to explore the possibilities of the MMA, and as the teacher and the administrative leaders prove what can be done with the aids, other teachers will take advantage of the resources.

Problems

Any number of excuses can be given as to why the MMA cannot assist in the learning process. Most administrators have heard comments such as, "Every time I need the equipment, it is inoperable," "I'm frightened to death of anything mechanical," "Students cannot be trusted to use the equipment independently." Doubtlessly, such experiences at one time or another have justified the comments. On the other hand, what has been futile on one occasion need not be futile on all occasions.

Whatever equipment is available must be maintained so the repair time is reduced to an absolute minimum. Schools which have used the MMA to great advantage for independent study have assigned a single staff member to the many responsibilities found in any program which makes wide use of technological tools. Teachers or students need equipment at a given time; when the equipment is not available, the consequences of a theoretically sound idea can be devastating.

Two or three alternatives are possible to eliminate, or at least reduce, the "mechanical monster" phobia. In-service education programs can be devoted to MMA training sessions for teachers. In addition the teachers or the MMA director can train students to use the equipment. In one school all students who have been checked out on various pieces of equipment are given cards which indicate that the student can use whatever apparatus is necessary. Student projectionists are often very helpful when it comes to assisting students on independent study. A number of workable alternatives makes a difficult situation operable.

Students *can* be trusted to be careful with the MMA. Unfortunately, in many schools the rules and regulations which govern the activities of the entire student body are formulated because a relatively small percentage of students are not self-disciplined enough to follow common-sense rules of conduct. The mass of good students is punished because of the minority of bad students. Some students may need to be supervised 125 percent of the time; therefore, it would seem unwise to have these students engaged in independent study activities. If the discipline-problem students are not self-directed enough to take advantage of the learning opportunities available to them, then the opportunities should be withdrawn from these students. However, the other students should not be punished for the misdeeds of the problem students. Most students realize what values are available to them via the MMA; therefore, the students take whatever precautions necessary to insure proper treatment of equipment. Experience in some schools has shown that students are usually more reliable than some teachers about reporting aids that need to be repaired. Also advancements in tools have helped to overcome the operation problem. Inexpensive viewers for slides and filmstrips, self-threading movie projectors, programmed texts, and cartridge tapes have reduced many of the operational handicaps.

Many schools have more materials available than they realize. Materials are located in many different rooms throughout the building; frequently teachers in one department are not aware that usable materials are available in another department. Unfortunately, this same condition may exist between teachers within the same department.

If schools are to make maximum utilization of the resources available, it is necessary to have all items cataloged in a central source area. The equipment, films, etc., may be located in many different places, but students should be able to locate the materials in the catalog and then use whatever items necessary. Frequently, the major source catalog is located in the library or the instructional materials center. Wherever the source is located, the students must have easy access to the files.

The MMA may necessitate special reviewing requirements, for example, darkened rooms and special soundproof areas. Sometimes the room-lighting problem can be solved by reducing the size of the projection image; a regular projector can be used in a lighted room if the picture is no larger than one square foot. For individual viewing, this process is often used. Outlet jacks on TV monitors, tape recorders, record players, and movie projectors can accommodate earphones which in turn eliminate the need for soundproof rooms. A well-trained A-V man who understands the concept for the use of the MMA in independent study, as well as being an A-V specialist, can do a great deal to reduce the inappropriate outlay of funds for unneeded facilities.

The Instructional Mix

The school that attempts to provide for individual learning recognizes the need for individual motivation as a basic feature of its program. Independent study places emphasis on the utilization of available resource materials. Students are guided by teachers who know what resources are available and how the material can best be used to help meet students' needs. When properly used, the MMA can help students discover new truths, synthesize generalizations, improve skills, and change attitudes. Tools so powerful should not be overlooked.

When staff members have clearly defined the goals of the school, the threat of gadgetry and gimmicks, which are sometimes inappropriately associated with the MMA because some salesman misrepresented a particular device, can be eliminated. The definition of goals is the first step; the function the MMA can play to help accomplish those goals follows. Inevitably, the technological products of the twentieth century which can help to improve the quality of instruction will find their way into the school's educational program. The use of MMA may be hindered by numerous problems, but the precise implementation of the MMA for individualized instruction, as well as for other parts of the total school program, must be determined. The products must be made accessible to all of the students who can assume the necessary responsibilities to gain from the learning experiences. Clearly, the quest for improved individual instruction include maximum utilization of the MMA. The effectiveness of the MMA for individualized instruction is positively related to the instrument used, the technique incorporated, and the materials presented. Certainly, no single piece of equipment can be expected to fulfill completely all of the needs of all the students. Materials can be both *effective* and accessible, but poor utilization by teachers and students may reduce the potential *effectiveness*. The media found to be most usable require constant effort to make them even more readily available.

Effective education depends upon effective communication. Clearly, the MMA can be effective communication tools. MMA seek to manage learning in an intimate, one-to-one sense and to assure that the student will, in fact, understand the concepts, principles, skills, etc., which the MMA attempt to simulate. Indeed the MMA may be thought of as private tutors for each student. The inherent advantages and potentials for improvement suggest that the expandable limits of use for the MMA is far from being reached in most schools. As progress continues in basic application of the MMA for individualized instruction, it seems certain that teachers will be able to redeploy their time for whatever uses they deem important; the redeployment of time becomes a possibility when the MMA are used to their fullest advantage.

Some individuals will continue to discuss, perhaps forever, the pros and cons for the use of the MMA in independent study. While these persons discuss merits, other individuals will continue to make practical applications.

CHAPTER 10

Facilities, Equipment, and Independent Study

by

JOHN H. BEYNON

*John H. Beynon is Program Specialist in School Buildings
for United Nations Educational, Scientific, and Cultural
Organization in Paris. Before joining UNESCO, he was a
staff member of the Educational Facilities Laboratories at
Stanford University and consulted with educators in all
parts of the United States in developing new buildings
and remodeling old ones. He has a degree from Massachusetts Institute of Technology in architecture. He contributed to* Study Carrels: Designs for Independent
Space, *published by the School Planning Laboratories at
Stanford University.*

THERE IS no single environment that is best, optimum, or ideal for
independent study. The variations are as broad as educational programs and as diverse as the members of any student body. The
overused architectural cliché, "form follows function," attributed to
Louis Sullivan, can be applied to facilities for independent study.
The first problem is to decide what will happen in the educational
program; the second is to find an appropriate setting.

Previous chapters have shown the diversity of educational thought
on the nature of independent study. The concept touches the elementary school student as well as the high school student and extends
from the humanities through language instruction through science
through vocational training. Too often designers have been directed

166

to create independent study space for programs that are vague in the minds of educators and usually not even in operation. The probability is that the teachers who are going to teach are not even available to the designer as a resource. The result is that the success or failure of the program is often left in the designer's hands. Because of the newness of the concept, he fails to understand it completely; and therefore, he is unable to contribute much genius to the design.

Thus the problem for the educator is to identify with some specificity the functions that will (or should) take place in the independent study program. The educator must see to it that his architect understands both the basic operations and the subtleties of the instructional program. How important are visual and acoustical privacy? Will students work in teams? Should the teacher be able to work beside the student? What kinds of materials will be used? How handy must they be? What electrical equipment might be used here? These are some of the important questions that need to be asked and answered by the educator before he engages an architect to begin building facilities for independent study.

From Whom Do We Learn?

Facilities are only a stepchild of education. The best programs can go on in the worst school buildings and the worst programs sometimes operate in the best spaces. India's former Prime Minister Nehru supposedly commented once that a teacher, a few students, and a Banya tree constituted a school. While it may be true that facilities neither are the essential part of a school nor are a guarantee of the quality of its program, still there is little question that well-planned facilities do help the teacher by accommodating students' special instructional needs. This is particularly true of independent study which is a sharp departure from the traditional workings of a school or even its library. Thus independent study requires particular facilities.

From whom, then, should the designer take his cues? One teen-ager is reported to have studied homework most intensely locked in the bathroom sitting cross-legged on the toilet stool using the flush tank for her desk and a running faucet as a provider of "acoustic perfume" to drown out the foreign household sounds. Of course, this solution is a bit extreme, but the objectives are all sound: since this was the bathroom and not the dining room it meant no one would stop by to talk; the running water provided acoustical privacy though in a manner reverse from our normal approach; and the yogi-like posture perhaps helped to keep her awake and concentrating.

Besides taking advice from individual students, there are several reasonably sophisticated surveys on student study habits which the designer might examine.[1] The significant conclusion of these is: the majority of students do not like to study in large rooms. Instead, they prefer small intimate spaces where they can work alone and without interruption. However, "human engineering" studies and analyses of the impact space has on learning are almost nonexistent. Until this information void is satisfactorily filled by reliable research, we are obligated to seek the best solutions we can with common sense as the guide.

Variety—The Spice of Space

Since privacy, both visual and acoustical, is considered important to a successful independent study program, the *carrel* which has long been found in graduate level research libraries has found its way into the American schoolhouse. This essentially means providing a student with a desk where privacy is provided by several panels that prevent the student from seeing things that happen around him. It also keeps others from distracting the studying student. It should also provide bookshelves, storage space, a file or whatever else the student may need to hold all the necessary tools for learning. As the lockstep system of traditional class scheduling crumbles away in deference to the flexible schedule with its twenty to thirty minute time modules, and as students are given an increasing amount of freedom to study independently, the school will become a beehive of almost constant and varied activity. The carrel can help make the flexible schedule acceptable and helpful to the student. Traditional tables and chairs simply are not a satisfactory answer to providing the environment for independent study.

Different students have different wants and different needs. All teachers and parents know that the bathroom environment mentioned earlier is not what all students will or should choose for their studying. Some will want music and not running water for background sound; some will prefer lying on a carpeted floor to sitting cross-legged on the toilet stool. There are even those few who will select a quiet place, a straight-backed chair, and a neat desk. Again the designer might do well to take a cue from those who will be using his carrels.

Students are not all shaped alike, nor do they learn alike. They do not all like the same kind of pizza, nor do they all respond positively to the same kinds of study spaces. Furthermore, if given a choice an individual student will select different environments for different kinds of studying. A recent interview with a junior college student by the community college planning center at Stanford University showed that one girl picked the library as a place for casual studying and meeting friends. But when time came to cram studying, she retreated to the music listening room and insulated herself from the outside world with a discretely disconnected headset. The headset, she found, was an insulation against disruption by other students.

The studies done on student preferences show this same pattern of variety of choice, but too often the results are misinterpreted. Generalizations and conclusions stress the needs and desires of the majority. Because of his concerns for visual unity and lower costs through bulk buying and mass manufacture, the designer is usually seeking a single neat solution and often gives one hundred percent of the students what sixty percent preferred sixty percent of the time. This kind of democratic excess can lead to abuses of individual advantage. A school which is dedicated to individualized instruction must be sensitive to the many preferences which individuals have in terms of learning spaces. Standardized facilities are not appropriate for individualized learning programs.

Besides the diversity of student desires, there is a variety of student shapes and postures which require various sizes and shapes of desks, chairs, and carrels. One essential notion of carrel design, is that of variety. But this is not to be confused with visual chaos. Any competent school designer will try diligently to furnish a school with elements compatible with one another and compatible with the building. And while the all-too-common repetition of elements is one approach to compatible design, it ignores the needs of the students. Good school design can be achieved with unity through diversity better than with balance through conformity. Today's school planners need to be concerned with the unique space requirements needed for independent study, even if it means that one room or space will not be like all other rooms or spaces. The architectural tendency toward congruence and the educational tendency toward standardization of facilities cannot continue if independent study programs are to flourish.

TV or not TV

Another consideration in providing a variety of carrel types is the nature of the educational program. If one essential purpose of independent study is to teach each student in the way he learns best, we can expect a variety of programs and, consequently, a variety of facilities. Some students love books and learn best from them. Others find teaching machines fascinating; still others will get the most out of a film or some other visually reinforced presentation. Carrels that will accommodate each of these approaches to teaching should be made available to all students.

There are people in education, as well as in advertising, who argue that "a single picture is worth 1000 words" and that "there is nothing that can't be taught by television." If these statements are true, then every carrel should be a miniature audiovisual center with a built-in television set. Such facilities can now be found at Grand Valley State College in Michigan and Florida Atlantic University in Florida. However, most public schools, have found either that they cannot afford to build for this approach or that adequate teaching materials are not yet available. One California high school estimated that a closed-circuit television system with one set for each four students and programs provided by a dialing system would add twenty-five percent to the cost of the school. The estimates for program and materials development were even higher and thus completely impossible without sizable outside funds.

Perhaps the most sensible approach is that taken at the RichMar school district near San Diego, California, which has designed a carrel capable of accommodating any of a variety of small machines suitable for independent study (see Figure 1). Since manufacturers are reluctant to develop products for unproven fields of limited scope, proper audiovisual equipment has been slow in becoming available.

More research funds are needed to develop bold new technological aids to instruction.

However, more reliable customers have come to the educators' aid. Those of us with home movies who cannot remember from one showing to the next how to thread the projector have spawned the self-contained film clip. Salesmen who want to give an audiovisual presentation out of their briefcase have caused compact rear screen projectors to be marketed. And lastly, the affluent American who wants to go both to the beach and stay home and watch the ball game on television has launched the small portable television set. The prices of all these items are low enough so that any school can, and probably should, have a cluster of carrels which can be used for any of a half-dozen portable machines which can be easily manipulated by students. Included among these are television, teaching machines, movie projectors, portable language labs, and rear screen projectors.

As soon as educators design learning materials which require these technological aids, the hardware will be developed by manufacturers. Already there seems to be more hardware available than learning materials to be used through them. Getting the various technological aids to instruction in the schools is a problem for the educators to solve.

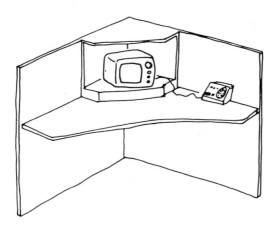

FIGURE ONE

Design

Most carrels are used for library-like study, but sometimes they are used with the addition of the mechanical and electronic aids mentioned above. Since one fundamental part of independent study is that of comparing bits of information from several sources, even carrels planned solely for book use need to be generously proportioned. The size recommended for college students is an area two by three feet. Elementary and secondary school teachers often find this unnecessarily large and use an area closer to twenty by thirty inches. However, there are also those who want carrels to be sufficiently large for a teacher and a student or for two students working together. In this case a carrel width of four feet is required.

The height will be determined by the size of the user. For adults this will be from twenty-eight to thirty inches. Any desk manufacturer has data for children. The best height for the isolation panels has been found to be sixteen to twenty inches and they should extend twelve inches beyond the desk's front edge (see Figure 2).

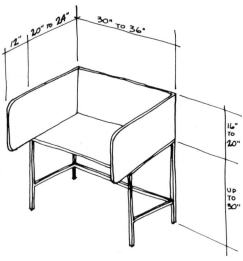

FIGURE TWO

While these dimensions are taken from carrels that have proven successful in the field, there are cases where one might choose not to follow them. For example, one school used a thirteen-inch panel height because they wanted the students occasionally to take instructions from a proctor. The twelve-inch side extensions might be reduced if the carrel is over three feet wide because students are further apart.

If audiovisual equipment is going to be used, a special place for it has to be provided out of notebook range to allow the student to take notes during the showing. It is best to put the equipment at eye level. If higher, the student may be looking into the ceiling lights; and if lower, it encourages poor posture.

Convertibility and Flexibility

One characteristic of a well-designed carrel is that it will not become obsolete as educational changes call for modifications in facilities. Since the independent study concept is new to primary and secondary schools and since educators are still experimenting with the concept, carrel design too is in a state of flux. By sticking to a basic system of components to make up carrels, costs can be lowered, and the carrels can be integrated into the building's dimension system. Through clever designing, a series of elements can be developed that fit a standardized module yet lend themselves to being assembled in several ways. In this way bulk purchase of units will cut costs and yet when remodeling time comes, they can be reassembled to fit the modified program (see Figure 3).

Even a simple idea such as divider panels that slide sideways or swing out of place can provide varying-sized spaces (see Figure 4). Also functional change should be planned for; what is today a library carrel, used only for reading, might become a student's private, television-equipped carrel tomorrow. This means that an individual carrel might in the beginning be only a table top with attached dividers; but it may one day have a book shelf, a file drawer, and a television set attached. Perhaps one way to approach such a design is to plan it originally for its most complicated form, then build it for the most simple (see Figure 5).

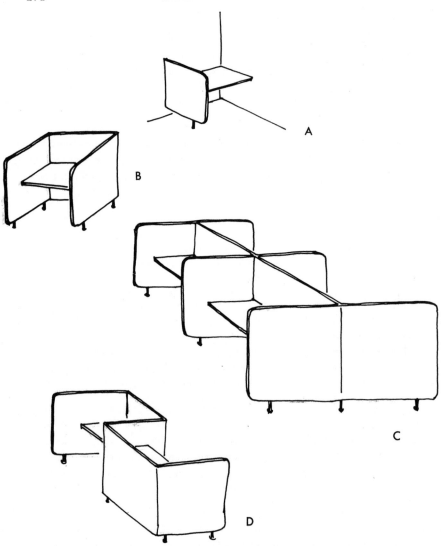

FIGURE THREE

The most frequently overlooked item is a chase for hiding the wires that link the carrel with the school's telephone, television, and electric power source. The exact location of the outlets will be determined by the nature of the wire chase and by whether or not the carrel stands free, is clustered, or is adjacent to a wall. But whatever the case, the outlet should be at least six inches above the table top,

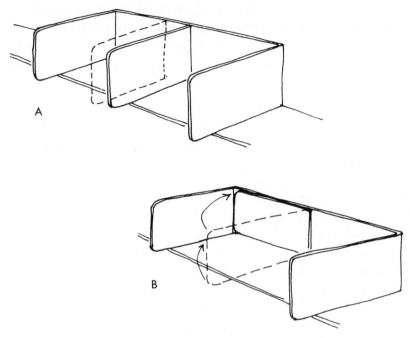

FIGURE FOUR

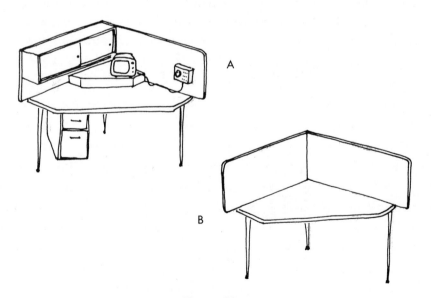

FIGURE FIVE

clear of notebooks and papers. If required, the telephone dial is best located a little above the outlets and on the right-hand side. The electrical box also should be capable of modification since electronic designs seldom stay in fashion over many years. Space left for future installation of new jacks or switches is a provision of the future.

Acoustics and Lighting

The carrel's acoustical treatment and lighting will depend on the design of the room where the carrel is placed. If the space is typical of most American classrooms with plaster or concrete block walls and an acoustical, tile-covered ceiling with strips of widely spaced fluorescent lighting, the carrel will have to be designed specially to make reasonably ideal study conditions.

While normal book reading is a quiet business, team studying and team use of machines with whirring fans and clicking devices are not. Of course, sounds that normally come from speakers can be channeled through earphones, thus isolating the noise and isolating the student. Within reason the other noises can also improve room acoustics by creating a masking noise that serves to obscure the more distinct sounds of conversation—much like the young lady's running water. But sound absorbing materials that cut down echoes should be added to keep reverberation time short. If the room does not have sufficient draperies, acoustical tile on the walls, or carpeting, then special absorbent panels should be added to surround the equipment as much as possible. Heavy screening over fibreglass batts often is adequate (see Figure 6).

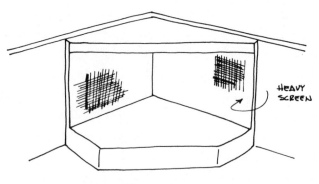

FIGURE SIX

The visual barriers will cast shadows from the strip lighting; and therefore, it is generally necessary either to change ceiling lights so that they approach being a luminous ceiling or add lights in each carrel. The chief virtue of the individual light is that it allows the student to adjust it to his own personal requirements. The chief drawback seems to be that it sometimes becomes the victim of curious students whose independent work wanders off the academic track.

Providing electricity to carrels where electronic equipment will be used is nearly a must; for while much equipment is battery powered, much still requires the standard one-hundred-ten-volt power source. This being the case, the added light is also a reasonably simple matter to provide.

The Manufacturer's Dilemma

Many educators wonder why, with the current emphasis on independent study, they cannot order a decently manufactured carrel from a catalog. It is important for them to understand the problems of the manufacturer in order to make attractive demands of industry.

Tooling up for any new piece of equipment requires a major capital investment, and industry is loathe to invest large sums in new designs that can be easily taken over by competitors. Design patents are so much less defensible than normal patents that companies usually prefer to overcome the competitor through pricing or advertising rather than lawsuits. This being the case, a low-quality producer can quickly take a good concept into which the first company has invested tens of thousands of design and prototype dollars.

The peculiar desires of clients have also left the manufacturer in a quandary. To date educators and architects have been seeking highly individual solutions. What is considered perfection for one school is vigorously rejected for another. This has often forced manufacturers to amortize both design and tooling costs with only several orders, forcing costs to be far out of line. The lesson to the educator is that if he is going to get a low-cost, high-quality, manufactured carrel, he must be willing to accept designs that have broad applications. Manufacturers will invest more money and energy in carrel design as the number of educators who demand them increases.

However, the educator may prefer to develop his own design in conjunction with his architect, mocking it up in the school shop. This was done with success at Lakeview High School, Decatur, Illinois. After making appropriate changes in consultation with the local cabinetmaker, the educator can have the carrels built locally at great savings in purchase price. While locally produced carrels may be all that a school district can afford, it has certain drawbacks. The re-

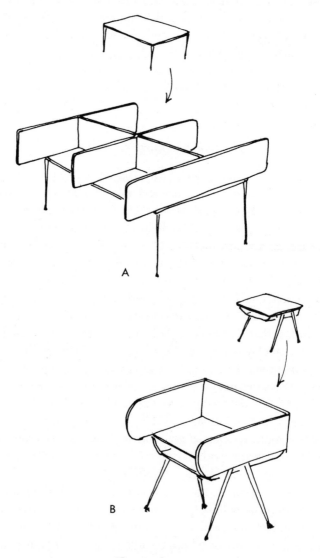

FIGURE SEVEN

search on both design and construction is homespun and probably not as sound as that done by the professional consultants used by the manufacturer. Also the manufactured product is usually better built and of better materials.

Many schools moving into an independent study program will already own a full complement of furniture and will understandably be hesitant to discard it and invest in new carrels. It is possible for them to remodel certain typical school equipment for independent study. Tables or desks for example can be made into suitable carrels by adding dividers (see Figure 7).

There is probably no need to go beyond the school shop or the local carpenter for equipment such as this. Also, small portable bookcases and storage units can be mixed with tables to provide carrel-like spaces (see Figure 8).

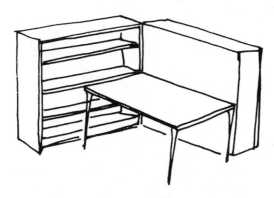

FIGURE EIGHT

Overall Planning

So far we have dealt only with the nature of the individual carrel giving little thought to where in the school it should go. For the most part, this is an educational decision, but it will be influenced by the building design too.

The library traffic pattern normally pulls students from the card catalog through the stacks to the study areas. By locating the study spaces at the room's edge, the carrels are taken away from the most active places. Perimeter location has an advantage for tapping into the school's electronic systems. It is less costly and easier to change wiring that runs through panel walls than that which is embedded in a concrete slab floor.

While some schools have chosen to line students up side by side facing the walls, others have objected that it is too confining. One serious drawback is that in this scheme every student backs on a

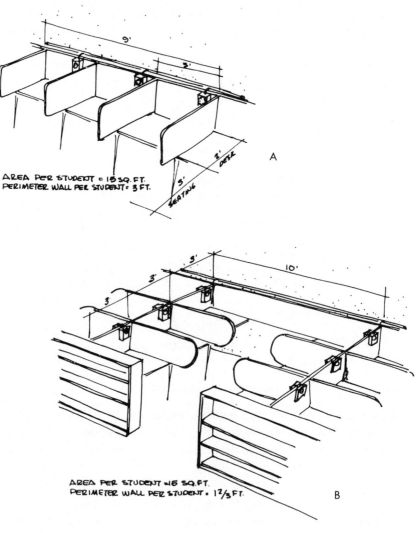

AREA PER STUDENT = 15 SQ. FT.
PERIMETER WALL PER STUDENT= 3 FT.

A

AREA PER STUDENT =15 SQ. FT.
PERIMETER WALL PER STUDENT = 1 2/3 FT.

B

FIGURE NINE

fairly major walkway. By using a peninsula scheme three or four students deep, it is possible to locate the student on a traffic cul-de-sac, giving him a better chance occasionally to focus on a distant point as well as getting more carrels at the perimeter for easy utility connections (see Figure 9).

But not all carrels can be placed around the perimeter of the rooms. When it becomes necessary to place them in the center, it is best to cluster several together, both to be efficient in the use of space and to make it possible to service several from a common electronic connector (see Figure 10).

FIGURE TEN

A minimum carrel with a student will take up a space three by five feet, larger carrels requiring a little more; the overall rule for estimating total area, including circulation space, is to figure twenty-five square feet per student.

These rules are valid for both large and small resource centers. However, one basic reason for establishing departmental centers is to get students and teachers closer to materials—which presumably includes tapes and films as well as printed matter. Decentralization of the school means either duplicating this equipment or making it portable. The often heard argument that bits of information can simply be dialed remotely from a central spot sounds both slick and modern, but in fact is not realistic at this time. Only a limited number of programs are available and the electronic components necessary to accomplish this feat are not available as an assembled unit. However, this kind of remote retrieval is certainly in the wave of the future.

Science Facilities

The special needs for science carrels are spaces to store both projects in progress and supplies for working on projects. Since laboratories are used by a number of class sections each day, projects usually have to be moved after each class to make way for the next student. Robert Lewis, science education consultant of Aspen, Colorado, has tackled the problem—at least for biology—from two viewpoints: first, for the class that may have five or six students per section working on special projects and, second, for the class where everyone is working independently. For the few independent students, Lewis developed a carousel carrel which has six stations, all served by several lazy susans which bring specimens, slides, reference books, and supplies at the touch of a finger. A special rear screen projection system enables the student to use a typical two-by-two-feet projector. Long-lasting projects are carried on elsewhere in the room, and this six student unit serves mainly as an analysis center.

For the class that has nearly all its students working on different projects, a perimeter scheme with a continuous counter was developed. The counter is divided into student stations, and each is specially equipped for a particular kind of work. While each unit has some space available for keeping long-term projects, others are stored in a special space adjacent to the laboratory or on shelves designed to hold cages, aquaria, plant boxes, and the like, but including the utilities needed for the lights, pumps, and heaters necessary to sustain plant and animal life.

Other Fields

Special facilities will need to be developed for each content field. While it may be wise to have a multi-use carrel for the student or for several students, specialized facilities will be necessary for some content areas. In addition to science, distinct carrels are needed for art and mechanical drawing. Some schools will want to develop independent work spaces in homemaking and industrial arts as well.

The space in a school needs to be planned so that it can maximize the individual efforts of the student, no matter what subject he is studying. No formula can be given for distribution of space among the content areas or between classrooms and study carrel areas. What has application for one school's program will be at odds with another school's requirements. Each school must set up its own educational specifications before building specifications can be drawn.

Responsibilities of Planning

When a school does not establish a set of specifications and goes ahead with a building program, the architect is put in the position of being the educator. In these cases it is the architect who is telling the educator how to shape a program of instruction. Too often insufficient time and creative thinking go into a building program.

As one thinks about a new school building, it is well to involve the local staff in the planning from the very beginning. At the same time, it is a good practice to secure the services of competent and experienced educational program consultants. Consultants can help crystallize thinking, clarify issues, and raise significant questions.

The Rest of the School Building

This discussion has centered largely around the independent study carrel as it relates to and stimulates independent study. Of course, a school must have many other kinds of spaces. However, the type of space needed for group instruction is to be determined by the other elements in the school program. For instance, some schools will want to use large-group instruction with their independent study. This will require rooms very different from those usually found in the traditional school. There may be a trend toward establishing a program of instruction which calls for small seminar groups as a part of the regular school organization. This requires a very different kind of room than the one we are so accustomed to seeing. At the same time, as the room's use varies and the size of the group changes, so does the furniture and equipment in it.

Perhaps the most promising innovation in the leading schools of today is the increase of the establishment of the Instructional Materials Center. This center combines the resources of the traditional book-oriented library and audiovisual aids department. It is larger than both, even when combined; and its operation is characterized by activity and diversity. Students do more than read. In the Instructional Materials Center they can type, construct, and discuss, as well as work on programmed learning, see films, and listen to recordings. The center is a supporting foundation for an independent study program.

Independent study spaces can be established in a school with any kind of program. The traditional schedule does not devote the emphasis or time to this activity that the flexible schedule does. However, the cornerstone of any independent study is the study carrel.

Other Than Carrels

This discussion has centered largely on the carrel because it is the fundamental requirement for an independent study program and because its addition to an existing structure is both easy to install and relatively inexpensive to add. Other independent study spaces should be provided in a school. For every kind of potential independent study activity, there should be a space. For instance, there should be specialized facilities for art, for typing, for science, and so forth.

Some schools have been fortunate in being able to convert existing areas for the special use of independent study. Re-used space can extend from small areas of existing classrooms to whole new facilities for the use of special student projects. For instance, in an art classroom dividers can be put up in the back of the room so students can work on independent study projects while formal classes are in session. The same kind of redeployment is possible in other areas as well.

The re-use of space is a course many educators will have to take in the event building additions are not in the offing. Creative uses of existing space can often be found if the teaching staff concentrates on finding it. It is helpful to secure the assistance of an architect to help develop schemes for finding new ways of using building space as the school's program requirements shift.

The construction of a new schoolhouse or the addition of independent study offers infinite possibilities, of course, for the addition of independent study space. It can be a mistake to assume that independent study will require more space. If a school devotes less of the school day to group teaching and more to independent study, then less space needs to be assigned to group teaching classrooms, and more is available for specialized uses of independent study. Good architects and creative educators have few bounds for their imaginations in designing independent study stations for each content area.

Tomorrow

As has been implied throughout this chapter, the future of independent study is as important to today's planner as any present educational practice. Since the architect must design buildings that can accommodate the changes of the next fifty to one hundred years in education, it is wise to consider the role of independent study since this is a means for individualizing learning. To look back fifty years and then forward fifty staggers the imagination. However, schools are only beginning their entrance into the electronic age, so it is impossible to see all of the kinds of instructional devices that will have an impact on learning. Television, teaching machines, and computers are probably those which will make the biggest differences. Today's schools need to be geared to these technological aids.

For example, the computer is visualized by some as being used by schools not only for simple record-keeping but for generating complicated flexible schedules too. Some people even see it working as a teaching machine backing up the teacher.[2]

As an information retrieval device, the computer may someday serve to make available in every school a vast amount of information not found in any school today. As a supplement to the regular school library, other information might be requested and brought in remotely over telephone lines or coaxial cable from regional or national information storage centers. Slides or movies likewise could be brought to the individual student by television on a scale we cannot appreciate today.

Another development might be the home study center. Linked to a regional or local information source, programs could be brought into the home at the convenience of the user.

It is when we consider these kinds of possibilities that the electronic carrel begins to make sense. We can see its potential for providing people with information that previously was unavailable. Thus conceived, it is more than only an expensive and complicated way of providing ordinary library services. But, being realistic, it is clear that these opportunities for learning and teaching are futuristic, and we will probably move to adopt this equipment by stages. It is wise for each school to begin now to take a first step. Additionally, even when the machines are inaugurated, pencils and books will not be expelled from school, only supplemented by other materials. The teacher will always be the pivot of good teaching. He will have all of these new tools to help him do a better job as he teaches students.

Thus the carrel designer need not feel ashamed to design spaces that allow students to use the kinds of materials most often found in today's schools, but he should also create carrels that will adapt to the electronic aids of the future. The future becomes the present in a short period of time!

CHAPTER 11

In-Service Programs for Independent Study

by

DAVID W. BEGGS, III

David W. Beggs has been interested in in-service education programs for most of his professional career as a teacher, high school principal, and assistant superintendent of schools. Graduating from Millikin University with both the bachelor's and master's degrees, he has done graduate work at the University of Illinois and Indiana University, where he currently is on the staff of the School of Education. His book, Decatur-Lakeview High School: A Practical Application of the Trump Plan, *was published in 1964. He is co-editor of the Bold New Venture series.*

THE SCHOOL ADMINISTRATOR has no wand. He is not a Merlin. The good things that happen in a school result from calculated effort after careful identification of purposes and means by which the desired ends can be achieved.

Worthwhile independent study programs which are to be used on a widespread basis in a school take time to plan and effort to bring into existence. While it may be true that some teachers do a good job of encouraging independent study as a result of their own inclination and natural talent, it is not likely that all teachers in any school will employ good independent study as a mode of teaching without the assistance of the school's administrator.

Educational tradition has not placed emphasis on independent study. Most teachers in the schools had little experience of this nature when they were students. Few professional education courses have dealt with both the rationale and techniques of encouraging independent study. When independent study has been used it has often been in addition to regular course work and independent of the program of studies, as it should become.

The responsibility of introducing the rationale and the procedures of independent study are generally left to the building administrator to carry out, if they are to be a planned part of the school program. A complete and systematic in-service education program is a prerequisite to establishment of independent study as a solid link in a program of instruction.

An in-service program for independent study is a long range enterprise if it is to realize its maximum effectiveness. Asking teachers to encourage independent study is an easy matter. Giving them the tools to implement it over a sustained period is another issue. Experience has shown that a school which places a high value on independent study needs to devote a healthy portion of its staff meeting time to the subject. Staff meetings are not enough. A varied program must be conducted within the school staff.

Administrators working in schools moving in the direction of the Trump Plan, nongraded organization, or flexible schedules will find advantage in the staff study of the independent study concept early in their program's development. Independent study can be encouraged and, to a large extent, carried on in a school with a traditional class schedule. The full advantage of independent study, however, may not be realized until a flexible schedule is operated. The nongraded organization is built on a cornerstone of independent study.

Getting the Staff Started

Perhaps the first staff meeting on independent study should be consumed with a definition of the concept, a presentation of the reasons for its use, and a description of model independent study programs. Once the topic has been introduced, it is helpful to divide the faculty into smaller groups for discussions. These discussions should center around an analysis of the ideas presented. After the discussion groups have had their opportunity to evaluate the concept and its rationale, it is helpful for the total group to reassemble and report on the areas of agreement and disagreement.

FACULTY INVOLVEMENT

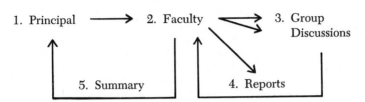

Before this first meeting is concluded, the principal, curriculum coordinator, or individual responsible for the session would provide the staff with a ready list of descriptions of independent study.[1] In addition, the topic for the next meeting should be announced. This might be a report from some of the staff on their readings and their observations about the concept.

During the second meeting the staff might begin with a review by some of the teachers of the previous meeting's discussion. An effort should be made to bring some examples of independent study the staff has used on occasion in their classes into the discussion. The more linkage with present practice possible, the easier it may be to move into new areas and extended use. While independent study practices have gone on in many classrooms, they have not often been the central method of teaching. Also the quality of some independent study has been low. The infrequency of use and the quality of the work will be apparent as the discussion continues. The wise principal will let this become obvious from the group discussion, not from his pronouncements.

At this point it might be well to begin a discussion on the value of independent study for less able learners. Few teachers fail to see the value for gifted students. Somehow almost everything seems appropriate for able learners. Often the rub comes in deciding that slow learners should do independent study. This consideration will be dealt with later. The point that needs to be made here is that the notion of independent study, unlike some instructional practices, is of value and has educational merit for all learners. There will be gradations of quality, of course, according to a student's ability; but this, as has been pointed out in previous chapters, is the power of the concept.

Each school will need to establish an operational definition and classification of independent study practices. Broadly defined, independent study is the method of teaching whereby students:

1. work on content often posed in the form of a problem or project,
2. get individual help from their teacher(s) as needed,
3. progress at their individual rate,
4. study topics at various depths and breadths, dependent on individual ability and interest.

Each of the infinite possibilities for combining these components of the concept needs to be considered by the staff.

Independent study activities can be classified in a variety of ways. Some gradations are determined by the complexity and applications of the content. Others are typed by quality and number of skills required for consideration. Still others are organized around the time given to them. The important issue for the staff to meet is what kinds of outcomes are to be sought. To get at this a classification of independent study might be considered.

CLASSIFICATIONS

Type	Level	Characteristics	Location
Content	First	Basic Processes; Rate Varies with Established Sequence; Reinforcement Emphasized; Scope Limited; Teacher-Determined Objectives	Classroom and Home
Content	Second	Basic Processes; Rate Varies with No Established Sequence; Stress on Usage and Application; Scope Limited; Teacher-Determined Objectives	Home and Classroom
Content	Third	Single or Multiple Concept Use; Rate Importance Diminishes; Stress on Rearrangement of Facts and Organizing Ideas; Teacher-Pupil Planning; Teacher-Determined Objectives	Classroom, Library, and/ or Home

CLASSIFICATION

Type	Level	Characteristics	Location
Content	Fourth	Focus on Broad Topics; Open-ended Possibilities; Student-Teacher Planning; Emphasis on Organizing and Reporting Ideas; Facts Used to Generalize; Student Objectives	Library, Home, Laboratory, Classroom, and/or Any-where
Skill	First	Elementary Skills or Concepts in Both Low and High Level Courses; Single Objectives; Emphasis on Listening and Reading; Scope Limited; Sequence Determined by Teacher; Quantitative Evaluation	Classroom
Skill	Second	Several Specified Skills Used To-gether; Objective is Task Oriented; Sequence Established; Scope and Complexity Varies; Teacher-Determined Objectives; Quantitative Evaluation	Home and Classroom
Skill	Third	Multiple Skill(s) Used; Broad Objectives; Student-Teacher Planning; Qualitative Evaluation; Open-ended; Teacher Advisors	Classroom, Library, and/or Laboratory
Time	First	Short Duration; Teacher Determined; Set Limits; Restricted to Class	Classroom
Time	Second	Limited Duration; Teacher-Student Planning; Deadline Set by Teacher; Restricted to Schedule	Home, Library, and/or Classroom
Time	Third	Elastic Duration; Student-Teacher Planning; Open-ended	Library, Laboratory, or Anywhere
Time	Fourth	No Time Set; Student May Meet with More than One Teacher; Open-ended	Anywhere

Making Group Decisions

Once the faculty has discussed previous practice within the school, reported and talked about the literature on independent study, and described independent study for the school, it is time to begin deciding about the school's independent study program. Such planning should include all the staff if the program is ever to be woven into the fabric of the school's operation. Decisions made on matters of teaching techniques must be made jointly by teachers and administrators. Care must be taken to insure wholesale participation in decision-making on such matters by all parties directly involved.

The accelerated use of independent study requires the school to reexamine some traditional practices. The techniques of teaching and student regulations in the school need examination. While the teaching techniques are more important, it may be wise to deal with the consideration of school regulations first. In the first place, retooling a teaching technique takes time, reinforcement, and is the more difficult with which to deal. In the second place, new teaching techniques are often more difficult and remote in staff consideration than

POLICY CONSIDERATIONS

Topic	*Options*
Content	1. Content Should Be Always Approved by Teachers
	2. Content Is Selected Exclusively by Students
	3. Controversial Issues Are Possible
	4. Controversial Issues Are To Be Avoided
Data Sources	1. Students Must Clear References with Teachers before Using Them
	2. Any Published Reference Is Permitted
	3. Non-School Consultants May Be Used on an Ad Hoc Basis with Teacher Approval
	4. Non-School Consultants Should Not Be Used
Excuses	1. Students Will Be Excused from School to do Independent Study
	2. Students Will Not Be Excused from School to do Independent Study
	3. Students Will Be Excused from Some Classes with Teacher Approval for Some Independent Study

POLICY CONSIDERATIONS

Topic	Options
Facilities	1. All Facilities And Classrooms Will Be Open to Students 2. All Facilities And Classrooms Will Not Be Open to Students 3. Some Facilities And Classrooms Will Be Open to Students 4. Students Will Not Be Excused from a Class Session
Group Meeting	1. Students May Meet in Small Groups at their Choosing for Study during the School Day 2. Students May Not Meet for Their Own Group Work during the School Day
Hall Passes	1. Hall Passes Will Be Discontinued; Students Can Move at Will to do Independent Study 2. Hall Passes Are Necessary for a Student to move about during School Hours
Hours, Library	1. Library and Other Facilities Will be Open Only During the School Day 2. Library and Other Facilities Will Be Open Evenings and on Weekends
Hours, School	1. The School Will Have Opening and Closing Hours which Approximate the School Day 2. The School Will Be Open or Keys Given to Students for Evenings and Weekends
Leaving School	1. Students May Leave School Grounds during the Day to do Independent Study 2. Students May Not Leave the School Grounds during the Day to do Independent Study without Parental Permission
Materials	1. The School Will Provide Extraordinary Materials and Supplies for Independent Study 2. The School Will Not Provide Materials and Supplies
Use of Equipment A-V, Bus. Machines, Home-making, Industrial Arts, Photographic, Science And So Forth	1. All Equipment in the School Is Available for Appropriate Student Use in Independent Study 2. No Equipment Is Available to Students for Independent Study 3. Some Equipment Is Available to Students for Appropriate Independent Study Activities

the mechanics of operating the school. Teaching practice changes will be dealt with in the last part of this chapter.

Some decisions have a higher priority in this area than others. Let's consider these. The changes in operational policies which may be required vary from school to school as deviations from normative practice are to be expected. Some of these and alternate options are suggested.

This list is a partial one, but the range of necessary considerations is shown. Policy does not have to be an either/or proposition, but might be positive for some students and negative for others. This, like each of the above, is a recommendation for the faculty to make to the administration. Perhaps it would be wise for it to go to the board of education for policy approval in some situations.

Independent study demands the inclusion of a variety of materials and approaches to learning. This variety may mean a student cannot stay in one place to carry out all or a part of an investigation. The first decision, then, is *where* and *when* a student will be allowed to use all of the school's facilities. Sensible bounds should be placed on the use of some facilities. For example, every student cannot go to one place at one time. The librarians, for example, may need more policies about the use of the library than a homemaking room teacher, simply because more students will need the library materials than the homemaking room facilities for work.

It might be advisable to make a chart of the school and designate the time the facilities are not needed for group instructional purposes. This begins to give the staff some idea of what periods of time space is available for independent study.

The next matter that must be dealt with is the use of hall passes or permission slips, movement of students from one place to another. As students see the purposes in going from one place to another, they will not be likely to abuse the privilege in moving about in the school. To some this notion may be surprising but experience has shown its soundness. It should be clear, however, that some students will abuse the opportunity to move about with freedom, particularly in the program's beginning if the school has been solid in rules on such matters. Sometimes the sudden acquisition of freedom results in a waste of student time. This possibility is, however, no reason not to take a step in developing independent study programs. Teaching involves a changing behavior. One of the values of widespread independent study is the opportunity it affords to teach students self-control and responsibility for their actions.

Having discussed procedural matters, it is appropriate to move into considerations of the substance of the independent study program. As has been pointed out in the first chapter, the in-service program is critical in effecting change in the school. The pace of the program should be regulated by the interest the faculty gives to the concept.

Models Proposed

During one staff meeting it might be helpful to ask the teachers to examine some model independent study projects. The models should be arranged so that some include open-ended possibilities with student determined outcomes and means. Others should include closed-ended types that may or may not be suggested by the teacher. The open-ended studies are of the kind suggested in detail in Chapter Twelve. They are organized around an original idea or topic and get into various views and interdisciplinary study. The closed-ended study has a logical point of termination. It is task oriented. The open-ended study is goal oriented.

As closed-ended study might be to explore the various systems of measurement used in the world. There are a set number of these systems. Only so much, although the quality of study and depth understanding will vary, can be explored in terms of the quantity of the topic. An open-ended study might be to investigate the effects of measurement on a selected reference field. First, measurement in ancient civilizations may be explored. The sequence may be chronological. Considerations can shoot off to various fields, artistic, literary, scientific, mathematical, and others may be considered. No bounds are set. The study's province is established by the student investigator.

The in-service program should be built in such a way that the content interests of all teachers concerned are considered. There is a possibility of danger when only one or two fields are used as reference models. English teachers should see models in their area. And home-making teachers should identify plans for application in their area. Experience has shown that social studies teachers can construct independent study models with more ease than mathematics teachers. Attention must be given to all of the areas in the school's program.

Stress on Student Involvement

The in-service program needs to stress the need for student involvement. This should not be restricted to involvement in a bulk of activity, but it should be involvement in isolating areas of interest and problems of concern.

While the use of independent study often calls for an interdisciplinary use of ideas and knowledge, it has a broader invitation. It opens up the opportunity for the student to pursue his interests, answer his questions, and deal with his concerns.

Teachers should discuss ways to stimulate the interest in the concept by students. The staff should discuss the place of conferences with students in this process. Guidance counselors should be involved in these discussions as they are often in tune with the unique concerns of each student.

For Some or Everyone

Independent study has value and a good chance of being beneficial for students of varying abilities. The notion that it is for the gifted is widespread but should be destroyed. Most independent study programs have gone on in this country in colleges and universities. With this identification and because bright students work well with almost any instructional technique, the image has been projected that individual study is for the gifted.

Slow learners can desire a full measure of personal satisfaction and knowledge accumulation on their level by independent study. These youngsters will not do the same quality as able learners. They are not doing equivalent work in group classes. The quality measure needs to be scaled to the student's capability, not to group norms.

Youngsters of limited academic ability should have the opportunity to pursue their interests, as well as the able learner. Students who hit learning plateaus early in their school years may never be able to move to a greater degree of skill proficiency. The school's job is to find this out and then provide learning activities which widen the range and increase breadth of knowledge and understanding.

The greatest hurdle to increasing the use of independent study for slow learners is the scarcity of materials which exists. Part of the in-service program's function might be to identify available data sources appropriate to students with a limited reading ability. Recordings, books, and magazines with a generous supply of pictures and group discussions are wisely suggested for these students.

Independent study is a means to increase the youngsters' interest in school. It is no wonder some youths leave school early. If the content of school study deludes a child, if he is met with failure at every turn, and if action-prone youth are asked to sit, sit and listen, listen to topics out of their sphere of interest or utility, why should they decide to stay in school?

Independent study needs to be geared to each learner. Group requirements need to go out the window. Individual challenges must replace them.

It is absurd to classify a complex human as being singularly bright or dull. While brightness or dullness usually is clustered, the degree of intelligence varies considerably within an individual in different areas of learning. The sum of human worth is not related to an intelligence index. This, few would deny. It behooves the school to find ways of developing human traits in whatever form and manner in which they exist.

One of the behavioral goals of independent study is to increase a student's responsibility for his own learning. No ability index is used to qualify this goal. Another aim of independent study is to teach a student to budget his time and to work productively. Here again the objective is not for any one but all students.

Teaching Techniques

This book abounds with reference to techniques of teaching needed to implement an independent study program. It would be aside from the purpose here to develop them in detail. It must be said, however, as the in-service program is discussed that planned consideration needs to be given to the canons of teaching that apply to independent study.

The teacher assumes several roles in developing these practices. Sometimes he is a data source and a source of motivation. Sometimes he becomes a counselor or advisor. At other times the teacher serves the student best by freeing him to pursue his own work.

New emphasis is placed on listening by the teacher. To help an individual, he first must be understood. Understanding of youngsters comes through listening, listening, and listening. Provocative questions enter into the interaction with the student.

The teachers will want to bring other teachers into the development of some studies. References may be made to other staff members for specific consultation on some points in an investigation. The in-service program must break down the notion that one teacher has a given select number of students. Any teacher in the school may work with any student in the school. All students are all the faculty's concern. It is, of course, true that the degree of responsibility varies for one teacher and some students. The underlying notion is that any students should be able and encouraged to get consultation and assistance from any teacher. Few teachers hope to be all things to all students.

Not only do subject competencies sometimes call for the use of more than one teacher, but some students will respond in a more positive manner to the teacher to which he may not be assigned administratively. There has been some hint in the teaching careers of almost every teacher that the degree of empathy varies from student to student. Why not maximize the human attraction of teacher and student or student and teacher in developing instructional programs?

Team teaching programs have the multiple use of teaching talent built into them. Team teaching calls for several teachers to work on a common instructional problem. This allows the ideas, skills, and knowledge of several teachers to focus on educational and student problems. It is believed that advantage will result from this staff effort for the students. Schools wishing to increase the use of independent study may wait to consider the advantages of team teaching. This is another valuable topic for the in-service program.

When, Oh, When?

When does a school find time for in-service programs? While progress can be made in after-school meetings, it is unfortunate if this is the only time that in-service programs can be conducted. After a busy, exhausting school day it is not realistic to expect some kinds of thinking and activities to go on. Teachers need larger blocks of time than can be arranged from the last bell to dinner to do some of the things necessary to develop first-rate programs.

While a school staff needs to meet after school on a regular basis, at least once a week, for staff study and planning, there should be plans made for summer workshops, released time during the year, and leaves of absence. During the warm summer days with no interruptions, teachers can make real progress in developing new programs and in improving techniques. Part of every good school budget should make provision for summer staff study and for released time for the staff to work on program improvements.

School programs do not improve by chance. They take time, effort, interaction, and the means to provide these. School boards which want to provide their students with *even* better programs must accept the responsibility to pay for this improvement.

This does not imply a school staff cannot take a tremendous stride during the year without workshops and released time. They can. In many places they have. The summer workshops and released time add to potential. Schools which want to move in the direction of inpendent study workshops for teachers would do well to demonstrate their interest by consideration during the school year.

One advantage of some team teaching programs is that they provide time during the school day for small staff meetings. This advantage needs to be considered as team teaching is discussed.

An Unending Process

The in-service program is never completed. Various phases or segments are concluded at different times. The principal worth his salt will identify a new province to conquer once one is finished. It is necessary, however, to return to some considerations from time to time to update practices and reconsider previous decisions.

Significant change in a school program requires evaluation as a necessary first step. Without some form of evaluation there is little reason for making adjustments. Improvement is the result of evaluation. Some evaluations are the business of all, others involve key members of the school staff. Major evaluations, undertaken for regional accrediting requirement satisfaction or for periodic total program assessment, are the noteworthy kind that consume attention in the literature. These are important at critical times in a school's development but the energy they take cannot be expended as part of an annual routine.

The routine of evaluation goes on daily. When the principal visits a class, an evaluation results. When a teacher chats with the principal in the hall or office, an unspoken evaluation is likely to be recorded in the teacher's mind. Principals and teachers will be able to summarize their evaluation of a school's independent study program almost any time. While highly subjective, it is still a valuable guide to action. Therefore, the princpal who is sensitive to the school's instructional program will know how the ship is sailing. He knows when and with whom to discuss one or another phase of the independent study program.

If independent study projects are failing to meet the goals of the staff, it is time to pause and take stock. Questions need to be asked, proposed solutions offered, and new approaches need to be tried. The dialogue between staff and administrators should never cease on instructional matters.

Some principals make it their business to conduct an annual survey near the end of the school year to gauge the sentiments of teachers and students about the total school program. The results are helpful in setting the course for the next school year's staff activities. Also, the results of this kind of evaluation are helpful to the district's chief school officer and to the board of education. When a school embarks on a new approach to teaching, it makes good sense to have fire insurance in the form of progress reports.

The Administrator's Role

The building administrator has many functions. As head of the school, he discharges the ceremonial responsibilities of crowning the homecoming queen and handing out the diplomas. If he did not attend to these matters, eyebrows would be certain to raise. More important and especially obvious if not done, the administrator is responsible for the program development of the school. What is taught and how it is taught is his primary business. Signing requisitions, selecting staff, and speaking to the parent groups are secondary to his leadership role.

Theories of leadership abound. Authority figures have been praised and defamed. Charismatic models have been judged the sign of the last century and the democratic head has been in vogue for some time. Emphasis needs to be on the *head*. A democratic school administrator is the head teacher, the responsible party for all that happens or does not happen in a school. As such, he must exercise his headship responsibilities in getting any independent study program off the ground.

Group processes are a part of his methodology but he does not transmit responsibility to the group for his own convictions and point of view. An administrator favoring independent study needs to be on record to this effect. This in no way means he tells teachers how to teach but it does imply he gives them positive encouragement in expressing judgments. The administrator is the teachers' teacher. He may select a few students with whom to work on independent study and share his successes and failures with the staff who are interested. An administrator who leaves the office from time to time and assumes teaching responsibilities, particularly with new methods, speaks with more authority and can be more convincing to the faculty.

Before teachers can develop potentials for independent study, the teachers must develop their own sense of security with the concept. They need to feel that it is all right if thirty youngsters are doing twenty different things in class. The administrator's continuing concern needs to be to facilitate the staff discovery that they can order varied learning activities.

Administrators encouraging independent study should encourage teachers to spread their domain outside the classroom. Teachers should be encouraged to talk with other teachers about what is and what is not happening in the classes. Maybe this is to be accomplished with formal teaching teams or maybe it is to be structured in staff meetings organized around content or grade levels. Children, too, need to be invited to leave the chalkboard walls to gather information and to work.

Team teaching, as has been pointed out in Chapter Four, encourages shared responsibility and, thus, cooperative planning. Independent study is most likely to be spread as shared responsibility is increased by a staff. The positive values of teacher helping teacher should not be ignored in considering team teaching as a tool to encourage independent study.

The Consultant

As a staff embarks on a new program, there is often advantage in bringing a consultant into the picture. A consultant can speak with an objectivity that regular members of the staff may not have. At the same time, the educator from the outside is viewed as a nonpartisan if stands are taken and views differ.

The consultants used by the school are not authorities in what the resident faculty should do. Hopefully a consultant would be an experienced educator with a wide range of experiences and theoretical orientation for the topic under consideration. His primary role is to clarify issues, thus enabling the staff to set a successful course of action.

Members of university faculties, state education departments, and neighboring school districts can be used with advantage as the in-service program develops. It is imperative, of course, that the consultant selected be grounded in the theoretical implications and versed in the practical methods of independent study.

Recognition Is Important

The teacher who does a creative job in instilling independent study as a mode of operation in a class should be recognized. Financial recognition is one kind and perhaps out of the immediate realm of possibility for building administrators. Another, and sometimes the most important recognition, is the personal kind given to the staff.

Why not ask the local press to do a story on Miss Jones and her students' independent study projects? What is wrong with including references to superior work done by a teacher in the school bulletin? Why should an administrator fail to tell a teacher how he feels about a good job students do in independent study?

If teacher initiative is to be expanded, it needs to be recognized. Changes may be needed in the school program and in sacred cows (as identified in Chapter Seven). This may even mean that a report is late or schedules are to be altered. The ultimate purpose of the school is to facilitate learning. The mechanics of administrative operation should not get in the way of the big goal. For this, among other reasons, a flexible schedule is suggested by some. Organize the day, say these advocates, to fit the independent study day, the time schedule to the independent study activities.

The use of a flexible schedule recognizes that teachers can and should make decisions about how and when students should learn. This is a bold concept with a new manifestation of faith in teachers. No longer do teachers bend to time requirements, time is molded to teachers' needs.

Rich Resources Are a Must

Rich resources are a must for a good independent study program. Students must have a variety of materials available. Materials vary in point-of-view, depth, reading difficulty, and emphasis. At the same time, there are various types of materials which can be used (as pointed out in Chapter Eight). The administrator must count it his responsibility to find out what teachers need for students and get it for them. No resource center can be a valuable aid to students if it is bankrupt in either breadth or depth of materials. The first order of business for the administrator as the school staff goes into an independent study program is to survey what is on hand and where voids exist in the school resources.

As a school goes into an independent study program, it may amaze some to see the new use the library and audiovisual collection gets by both teachers and students. Faculty meeting time may be sometimes devoted to allowing the staff to study the school's library holdings. Teachers cannot direct students to a data source if they do not know it is at hand.

In schools where the librarian has made the selection of materials for acquisition, a change is in store as the independent study program develops. Teachers will make suggestions, sometimes demands, for adding to the school's holdings. Here again the use of widespread independent study is involving the teacher more in the school's operation. Some schools have established means whereby students in high school can make suggestions about additions which need to be made in the collection of the reading and visual materials.

Some independent study projects may find their way into the regular school collection. A depth study of a topic by a student may be a valuable resource for others. School administrators must be alert to ways to increase both the functional quality and quantity of the total resources of the school.

Many schools could double their annual expenditures for materials and still not provide the range of materials needed. Reports to the board of education, talks to parent groups, and other reminders to the community of the demand for a rich storehouse of learning and reference materials should be made.

One day an enterprising publisher may bring out a book bound with an attractive cover which has no printing on any pages. This may be the biggest boon to education since the printing press was invented. This will be a do-it-yourself book. The student will select the topic, organize the ideas, and present them. Of course he will want to use ink filled books but this will be his book, his work. The day this happens, independent study will have reached an undreamed of stature of maturity.

This ends as it began. The administrator has no wand. He is not a Merlin. The good things which happen in a school result from calculated effort after careful identification of purposes and means by which the desired ends can be achieved.

CHAPTER 12

The Administrator's Role

by

EDWARD G. BUFFIE

*Edward G. Buffie has been an elementary school teacher
and principal in Park Forest, Illinois; junior high school
principal and curriculum coordinator at the Indiana University Laboratory School; and a professor in the School
of Education at Indiana University, where he is currently
associated with the teacher training program. He received
his bachelor's degree from Northern Illinois University,
his master's from Northwestern, and his doctor's from Indiana. In addition to being co-editor of the Bold New
Venture series, he has written some of the materials for*
Sets, Numbers and Numerals, *published in 1964.*

ELEMENTARY and secondary school administrators constantly receive demands, suggestions, and requests for changes in their respective programs. Time and time again the administrator, particularly
the building principal, is told he must accept the key leadership role
in bringing about desirable change in the instructional program.
While teachers can bring about certain kinds of improvements within
the classroom, administrative leadership is needed to spark basic
changes, the kind which will bring about significantly better instructional programs. This leadership responsibility has been properly
assigned to the principal. He is the agent who works intimately with
all the staff. He is the one who can encourage, assist, or prod teachers
into new instructional programs.

Out of all the fervor of educational activity in the past decade,
one idea emerges: more concern must be focused on individual learn-

ers and unique learning problems. Professional literature and the considerations of annual meetings of administrators' associations evidence this new focus.

Interest in innovation is in the tenor of the times. There seems to be a national commitment to the exploration of the new and exciting ways of changing, of redeploying and, presumably, of improving all phases of America's economic, social, and political life. Also, the instructional program has come under the influence of this change. In general, teachers and the lay public are more receptive toward educational innovation than at any time in the previous history of American public education.

Today many new approaches to teaching, not possible a decade ago, may be implemented with relative ease if administrators only identify and carefully introduce them. The means to establish new programs are easier to marshal than in the past. Boards of education across the country have demonstrated a willingness to spend money for workshops, materials, and equipment to an extent unknown ten or even five years ago. This new approval for funds manifests a public interest in even better education.

But what kinds of stimuli will contribute most toward the substantial improvement of our schools? Additional staff, more materials, increased facilities will not be enough to bring about fundamental improvement. Helpful as these resources are, the demanding requirement for increased quality needs the employment of better techniques of instruction and gearing instruction to each individual student. The concept of independent study is a means for providing this increased quality.

In implementing this type of learning experience a principal must work with his staff on program improvement. Thus the administrator should look at the various innovations which may be useful as part of, or related to, independent study programs.

Six Areas of Change

Change in School Organization. Tremendous attention has been given nongraded schools, dual progress plans, continuous learning plans, and flexible scheduling practices. Professional secrets fifteen years ago, each of these concepts has become widely publicized in educational literature. Each of these reforms is similar because each requires changing the self-contained classroom organization of education.

It is impossible to discuss the organizational, change-oriented programs without also discussing independent study. Independent study is a basic element of each. Students are to be given time and the stimulus to work on their own in each of these plans for organizing learning.

Changes Regarding Teacher Roles. During the early 1930's there was a marked departure from the self-contained classrooms which were formerly prevalent. Departmentalization took hold at all levels of public education from the first grade through high school, but then it faded in the elementary school and became firmly entrenched in the high school. Soon the Core Program evolved; and, of course, this necessitated another change in the role of the teacher. Thus, the teacher's role included concerns in several content areas and encompassed the added responsibility for satisfying the day-to-day interests of students.

With the use of team teaching the teacher's role has again changed; and perhaps this is the most exciting, potentially the change to have the greatest impact on instructional improvement. Team teaching is closely associated to independent study. In this role the teachers work in teams with groups or individual students to develop self-assumed student learning activities.

Change in Composition and Size of Class Groups. American educators first advocated homogeneous grouping and then they promoted heterogeneous grouping. They felt that the ideal group size was reached when a school had a ratio of one teacher for every twenty or twenty-five students.

Lately the concept of varying class size has been introduced. In this concept the size of the class is determined by the purpose of the particular instruction. When students are engaged in quiet activity, they are in large classes of up to several hundred children. When they are engaged in active participations they are in small working groups. Still at other times they are free to work on their own or in small groups on independent study. These changes in the size and composition of class groups are a part of many team teaching and flexible scheduling programs.

Changes Related to Educational Technology. In many schools technological aids have been introduced with positive reactions from teachers and students. Independent study can not be disassociated from the development of programmed learning, television, learning laboratories, and other technological tools. There is a major trend toward individualizing instruction through use of language laboratories and teaching machines. The time students spend in large television classes buys the time for small-group instruction and independent study.

Changes Related to Content. Major undertakings are currently underway in various subject-matter fields, particularly in mathematics, foreign languages, and science. Also English and social studies are being reviewed carefully. What impact or relationship independent study may have upon the new content is dependent more upon changes in goals and methodology on the part of teachers than on content. Significantly many texts and programs present a wide variety of work for students to do individually. Instead of one assignment for all students, graded assignments are suggested.

Change Associated with Method. Teachers are more apt to change their methods and techniques as goals and purposes undergo critical analysis and adjustment. It is granted that independent study is a method of learning and a device which teachers have used over the years, in one form or another. However, there is a new emphasis on the concept of independent study. Instead of a supplementary teaching device, it is becoming an institutionalized approach to teaching and learning.

Summary. Even a cursory glance at the six areas described briefly above makes it apparent that independent study is a major educational innovation. How then should administrators attempt to develop independent study programs in their schools? By introducing flexible scheduling into their schools? By introducing advanced technology or team teaching into their schools? There are many ways, but the essential element in any change must center upon the contribution this change makes toward the improved education of the individual. In elementary and secondary school programs the use of independent study is one of the ways to develop the potentials and interests of the learner and to help him toward content mastery. In every school it is the building administrator who is the agent for constructive change.

The Need for Independent Study

Beliefs and Practices: Some Strange Inconsistencies. It is hardly necessary for educators to make long lists of educational tenets and then call for reexamination of them. It is recognized that the things the school does are not always in concert with their stated aims or objectives.

For instance, who would question the following statement? Each child should have the opportunity to develop his potential to whatever extent possible. Each individual has his own unique pattern of growth and development. In every group of learners, there exists, without exception, wide differences in each child's potential, past achievement, desire, and motivation to learn. Yet many of the school's practices deny that youngsters are unique. Single curriculum prescriptions, standard learning assignments, uniform grading, and promotional practices deny the belief that individuals have differing capacities and abilities.

Taking a Look. Some school administrators have laid the foundation for examining independent study programs by first presenting to their faculties some very basic test data regarding the children in their schools. This data shows the range which exists within a group. By using the school's own test data, the disparity of abilities is pointed on a personal basis. Such an approach has merit since teachers identify quickly with their own school's students. For example, one elementary school principal organized his test data in the following manner:

IQ DATA FROM THREE
FOURTH GRADE CLASSES

Group	Intelligence	Test	Scores
	Group I	Group II	Group III
High	122	145	129
75%	109	125	103
Mdn.	104	117	92
25%	100	106	82
Low	91	96	70
Range	31 pts.	49 pts.	59 pts.

ACHIEVEMENT DATA FROM A TYPICAL
FOURTH GRADE CLASS

	Reading	Language	Arithmetic
High	8.7	7.9	4.9
75%	6.4	6.6	4.3
Mdn.	4.7	4.6	3.9
25%	3.9	4.0	3.7
Low	2.9	2.7	2.8
Range	5 years 8 mos.	5 years 2 mos.	2 years 1 mo.

Data organized in this fashion will evoke a reaction on the part of the faculty. Such information may be prepared for every grade level in the school. Teachers will be amazed at the tremendous individual variability within each group of their students which increases as children move from earlier to later school years. Variations of youngsters regarding their learning potential and past academic achievement are often not as pronounced as an analysis of differences in socioeconomic background. Indications of personal characteristics such as security, self-confidence, self-perception, work-study habits, and attitudes yield another dimension of marked human difference. Thus establishing the wide diversity between youngsters is not a difficult task.

In light of all the evidence one can marshal, faculty discussions may be directed toward this question: "What are we presently doing to provide for individual differences of our students?" Universal practices within a school regarding marks, graded textbooks, common courses of study for all children, retention policies, and so forth are antagonistic to the variations between youngsters. It is relatively easy to have one rule, one policy, and one standard. The logical demand in accounting for individual differences is for varying practices, many regulations, and differing requirements to compensate for needs among any group of learners.

Discussions of individual differences often center on what is to be done for *group* differences rather than for individual variations. Since in nearly every area of curriculum the schools are organized around groups, elementary teachers often talk about children only in the context of their reading group membership. There are groups of slow learners; there are groups of gifted students. Secondary school educators are more apt to talk about honor sections, vocational groups, college preparatory groups, and track groups. Seldom, in either case, is there enough focus on the individual as an individual within any of these classification systems.

What can be done to promote individual growth and accomplishment? One answer is to employ independent study as a mode of learning. At the same time, the school administrator needs to search and reappraise the policies and procedures under which students function while in school. The schools need to get rid of the single track, one-policy conformity in ordering the educational organization. Schools need to give customized instruction and original educational help for every student. The group must be replaced by personal considerations and individual learning prescriptions. Administrators need to reappraise school rules in implementing an independent study program since regulations must suit individual and not group needs.

Process and Content Goals

Educators in the field are not always aware of the changing emphasis educational theoreticians give to various aspects of the teaching-learning process. While there will always be a debate about what is desirable in a school program and what the outcomes should be, there is new attention being given to how the student learns rather than to what he learns.

For example, Glenn Heathers has identified three major sets of goals which are sharp, broad, and current with accumulated theory:

1. *The content goals*—included here are such things as: the learning of terminology, classification, information, explanation theory, and technical application of information and theory. You will note that the first three concern themselves primarily with the teaching of information or facts.
2. *The process goals*—instead of stressing acquisition of particular bodies of knowledge or content, emphasis is placed upon teaching students how to acquire, interpret, evaluate, and communicate knowledge. The tool skills, critical thinking, inquiry, *self-evalua-*

tion, development of personal interest, and study habits receive central emphasis.

3. *The personal-social goals*—these relate to such things as values (social, esthetic, theoretical), personality makeup (emotional security, positive self-concept, self-assertion, etc).[1]

Thus content is currently being viewed by theoreticians as a means toward an end. Learning products as measured by achievement test scores were once given a high value in evaluating educational progress. The ability to use these products was assumed to be a direct follow-up from knowledge. Definitely the trend today is to place emphasis on teaching students how to use ideas and develop concepts. Examination of the newer programs in science, mathematics, and social studies will validate this assertion. Emphasis is upon the search, the discovery, the investigation, or the process of inquiry. Students are led to search for interrelationships, patterns, and structures of ideas.

Independent study is the vehicle for students to use in reaching the process understandings the school designates as important. The accumulation of information and storage of facts should be given less stress than basic understanding of broad ideas. This is not to say that content is not important. Content acquisition is essential as a tool to use in the development of process understandings; however, it is not an end in itself. Often educators go too far in the direction of teaching only facts or in the other direction of teaching only unsupported generalizations. A balance is required for a useful and enduring education and this balance is established by the school administrator.

Implementation Procedures for Elementary and Secondary Schools

In the educational reform movement of today, independent study has been identified as a key element in some major innovations. The development of high-level independent study programs may be either a faculty endeavor or connected with the team teaching, nongraded school organization, or flexible scheduling practices. Each school must decide the best type of organization for instruction in its own situation.

While the newer innovations in organization have had advantage for some school groups, they may hold no advantage for others. The concern of a school's leadership must be to survey the literature, consider the alternate options to action, and select the most appropriate procedures for learning for its own school.

This leadership in a school is typically centered in the administrative council, composed of the principal, the assistant principals, and representatives of the faculty who are team leaders, department heads, or elected faculty representatives. This group often has decision-making influence if not power. They determine the strategy for bringing about changes in the teaching procedures used in a school. School boards, teachers, lay committees, and community members have influence upon the administrative council, but the council should be aggressive in seeking better ways to teach and in finding more effective ways for students to learn. The principal, as chairman of the administrative or faculty council, has to unleash the energies and creative abilities of this important group. Because of the time and sheer size of the group, the faculty cannot consider in depth all of the issues that come before the administrative council.

Once the administrative council agrees that youngsters should have the opportunity to develop their potential to whatever extent possible in independent study, they must develop careful plans to make the goal a reality. If they assume that there are possibly better ways of teaching and learning, then they must develop a faculty procedure to identify and implement these ways. The staff must be well represented in the advisory and decision-making council to assure the success of a new program or procedure.

The Work of the Administrative Council

Preparation and planning must be done at the administrative council level before any changes are made in the school's procedures or organization. Many questions need to be resolved. Among these are:

1. In the development of independent study programs, will team teaching, nongraded school organization, flexible scheduling, and/ or programmed learning be utilized or will the concept be developed in the traditional classroom organization?
2. What approach should be used with the faculty to develop the need for increased emphasis on independent study and to increase focus on the individual differences of learners?

3. How will the faculty be approached in regard to the proposed exploration of the independent study concept?

4. Should all of the school be involved in the initial use of increased independent study? Among the teachers who emphasize this procedure, must they all approach it in the same or nearly the same way?

5. What provisions will be made for teachers to prepare and study ways to use this new procedure?

6. Will all pupils participate in independent study programs? If not, how should the participants be selected?

7. What role should the school board or parents play in this venture?

Questions like these could be endless, and it is the duty of this council to identify questions, as well as pose answers.

One problem which occurs is that too often new projects are undertaken before the administrative council itself has a thorough understanding of what the task at hand involves. Without complete understanding, it is unlikely that the innovation itself will ever take firm root. Several years ago in a large midwestern city it was decided to nongrade all the primary elementary grades (first, second, and third years). The following fall all schools in the city were to be nongraded in these years of schooling. Even though a central office ruling was handed down, three years later the graded organization was used again. Why? Primarily it was because the elementary school principals and the teachers did not understand the philosophy which undergirded the nongraded school. Hence they were not able to assume their leadership role in an effective or successful manner. Understandably teachers and parents were confused. These new programs are doomed to failure from the start if those involved do not fully accept the need and understand the procedures of the new program.

Adminsitrators need to prepare carefully and read widely in the areas of an anticipated change. Consultants, university professors, and experienced practitioners with the innovation should be contacted for the contributions they can make to the local school program. Often state departments of instruction and national professional organizations are helpful in locating resource people.

Consultants, Meetings, and In-Service Programs

Administrative meetings should be held regularly for the purpose of planning program development and evaluating it once it is underway. In a sense, these activities constitute in-service growth for the administrator. Talking about in-service programs for teachers without reference to administrators' in-service development is short circuiting the way substantial improvement in a school takes place. Without knowledgeable and well-informed administrators widespread educational improvement is not likely in a school. Attendance at local, state, and national professional meetings by the principal can be an effective means of supplementing reading and providing a backdrop for constructive action. The trend toward establishing administrator's study councils, where a group of administrators voluntarily join together for professional investigation and share ideas, is a sound practice. It is well worth the time and effort it takes.

Working with Teachers

Once the foundation work in the administrative council has been completed, it is time to begin a full-scale faculty in-service program. The ultimate success of an independent study program or any other innovation rests upon the feeling of ownership the staff has for it. Sometimes administrators move into programs prematurely. It is disastrous to be overanxious with zeal for immediate change and telling tangible results. Working with teachers to nurture new attitudes takes time. Success of an administrator is measured in part by the staff's understanding of his role. The articulate administrator who works effectively with a staff is supple and is patient. The in-service program is the administrator's vehicle for program development.

The following is offered as a model for the administrator of the steps to take in implementing an independent study program:

1. Establish the need. This may be approached in a variety of ways, as discussed earlier.
2. Examine present practices. This will provide a common background. Discussion will flow quite freely on current practices. Both their strengths and weaknesses should be dealt with.
3. Introduce and explore new possibilities of independent study.

Descriptions, changing objectives, levels of independent study, changing role of teachers and learners, and administrative procedures to be effected must all be considered.

4. Set up target dates and designate individual responsibilities. A plan with bench-mark dates is helpful in establishing a target.

5. Determine implementation of program. During the early stages of the program, it is absolutely vital for the administrator to have close personal contact with the pupils and teachers involved. He must be available and willing to do whatever is necessary in order to assist in making adjustments from old to new modes of operation.

6. Schedule progress reports. Progress reports should be made about the program at regular intervals to the staff, the Parent-Teachers Association, the board of education, and the public. Programs need to be modified from time to time. These alterations in procedures should be discussed and reported widely.

Administrators should provide faculty members with a constant stream of selected materials. Articles, excerpts from books, test data, and the like will serve to stimulate thinking. Administrators should keep in close touch with faculty attitudes and judgments. The teacher is the administrator's counselor as a new program is being developed. Personal conferences on an informal basis should be used to discuss the program, its strengths and its weaknesses.

Providing the stimulus to a staff to consider large-scale use of a high level of independent study is only part of the principal's job. In addition, he should help create an atmosphere where it is all right to be wrong. More important, teachers should feel free to admit and share their judgments as to why some techniques do and do not work. If unsuccessful teaching practices must be kept in the shadows by teachers, the profit of mistakes will not be realized in a school.

Creative teaching is more likely to take place in schools where the principal does not concern himself with the scrutiny of each act or incident a teacher incites. Teaching is every bit as much of an art as a science. As an art some aspects of the teaching process do not have dictums. As a science teaching does have procedures and broad principles which are to be followed. A good administrator must be cautious about inadvertantly stifling the art while evaluating the science of instruction. The administrator is legally responsible to the board of education for the evaluation of the staff. This responsibility requires a full range of criteria considerations. Administrators are likely to see better teaching on the whole when they do not hinder individual initiative by overemphasizing their evaluate responsibilities.

As an educator visits a number of schools, it is apparent that some places are potentially more productive for innovation and experimentation. In these places concerns are openly and easily expressed. Candor can be used in discussion of the teaching process. These places are a result in part of an administrator who is receptive to the ideas and hunches of the faculty. In these situations the administrator is perceived as a willing partner, not a cold judge of teaching.

Since no school probably will ever have a surplus of creative teachers, an administrator can nurture creativity in teaching. He does this by giving approval and attention to practices which deviate positively from the norm. This approval is given in countless small but important ways. References in staff bulletins and meetings, personal conferences, newspaper reports, and visits to classes are good ways to let the notion be established that inventive, creative teaching is desired.

Rules May Go

It may be necessary to eliminate long-cherished rules as a staff works on program improvement. The cry that "we've always done it this way" is no barrier itself to *modification of operational policies*. Policies and procedures should be changed as the program's demands and the faculty's desires dictate.

Who said students need to have a corridor pass to get from place to place? Maybe it is in the best interests of productive learning to free students to move about according to their needs rather than according to the jangle of a bell. If some students do not operate satisfactorily with unbridled freedom of movement, why should restrictions be put on all students? These questions and others need to be debated and decided by all the staff. There are others, perhaps more important policies, which need review. These are related to course requirements and content areas. The point is that if a policy does not serve individual advantage, it should be reviewed for possible modification. The administrator has to set the tone and provide the means for these dispensations.

Selected Bibliography

PERIODICALS

Barzun, Jacques. "Keeping Abreast of Education," *Phi Kappa Deltan* 38:222, February, 1957.

Baskin, Samuel. "Experiment in Independent Study," *Journal of Experimental Education* 31:183-185, December, 1963.

———— and Keeton Morris. "Academic Round Table—The Use of Independent Study Programs," *ibid.* 33:103-106, February, 1962.

Beggs, David W., III, and James L. Olivero. "Place Out of Space . . . The Independent Study Carrel . . . and a Variety of Studies in Lakeview H.S., Decatur, Illinois," *National Association of Secondary School Principals Bulletin* 46:192-202, January, 1962.

Blancett, Frances L. "A Study Hall . . . Without a Teacher," *Kentucky School Journal* 42:38, January, 1964.

Bohning, Elizabeth E. "Independent Study of Literature in Translation," *The Modern Language Journal* 43:87-89, February, 1959.

Bonthius, Robert H., F. James Davis, and J. Garber Drushal. "Independent Study Programs," *Journal of Higher Education* 25:411-416, November, 1954.

Brown, Lois A. "The Chart System," *Journal of Education* 78:244-248, May, 1946.

Bunting, Mary. "Radcliffe Institute for Independent Study," *Educational Record* 42:279-286, October, 1961.

Chase, Dave. "The School Library as an Instructional Materials Center," *Peabody Journal of Education* 41:81-85, September, 1963.

Chickering, Arthur W. "Dimensions of Independence," *Journal of Higher Education* 35:38-41, January, 1964.

Congreve, Willard J. "Learning Center . . . Catalyst for Change," *Educational Leadership* 21:211-213, 247, January, 1964.

————. "Toward Independent Learning," *North Central Association Quarterly* 37:298-302, Spring, 1963.

Dixon, Fred B. "Independent Study—A Do-It-Yourself Program in English," *Clearing House* 36:556-558, May, 1962.

Emmerling, Frank C. "Salt for Education," *Educational Leadership* 21:231-233, January, 1964.

Faust, Clarence H. "The Accommodation of Superior Students," *Education Digest* 22:6-9, January, 1957.

———. "Rising Enrollments and Effective Use of Faculty Resources," *Association of American Colleges* 43:257-265, May, 1957.

Gladstein, Gerald A. "A New Approach for Identifying Appropriate Individual Study Behavior," *The School Review* 71:158-169, Summer, 1963.

Griffin, William M. "The Wayland, Massachusetts, High School Program for Individual Differences," *National Association of Secondary School Principals Bulletin* 47:118-127, March, 1963.

Hayward, Sumner C. "New Approaches to Collegiate Liberal Arts," *Liberal Education* 45:227-241, May, 1959.

Heller, Melvin P. "Outmoded Study Halls Give Way to Learning Centers," *Clearing House* 38:321-323, December, 1963.

Huffmire, Donald W. "Analysis of Independent Study Projects," *Science Teacher* 29:31-39, April, 1963.

———. "Criteria for Independent Study Projects," *ibid.* 28: 32-37, May, 1961.

Jackson, D. C. "Needed: New Life in the Colleges," *School and Society* 30:415-418, September, 1929.

Jackson, David M. "A Search for Practical Means of Improving Instruction by Increasing Students' Responsibility for their own Learning in University of Illinois High School," *National Association of Secondary School Principals Bulletin* 43:233-239, January, 1959.

———, W. L. Shoemaker, and Paul Westmeyer. "University of Illinois High School, Urbana, Illinois, Experiments Further with Independent Study," *ibid.* 45:198-208, January, 1961.

Johnson, Mauritz. "Needs for the Sixties," *ibid.* 47:3-12, February, 1963.

Kallen, David J. "Inner Direction, Other Direction, and Social Integrative Setting," *Human Relations* 16:75-87, February, 1963.

Keller, Charles R. "Call to Revolution in the Social Studies," *College Board Review* 44:13-16, Spring, 1961.

Koenig, Kathryn, and W. J. McKeachie. "Personality and Independent Study," *Journal of Educational Psychology* 50:132-134, June, 1959.

Krohn, Mildred L. "Learning and the Learning Center," *Educational Leadership* 21:217-222, January, 1964.

Leuba, Clarence. "Using Groups in Independent Study," *Improving College and University Teaching* 12:26-30, Winter, 1964.

MacDonald, James B. "Looking at Centers for Learning through Research-Colored Glasses," *Educational Leadership* 21:249-261, January, 1964.

McKeachie, W. J. "The Improvement of Instruction," *Review of Educational Research* 30:351-360, October, 1960.

MacKinnon, Donald W. "The Nature and Nurture of Creative Talent," *American Psychologist* 17:484-495, July, 1962.

Marland, Sidney P. "Winnetka's Learning Laboratory," *Educational Leadership* 20:459-465, April, 1963.

Mednick, Sarnoff A. "The Associative Basis of the Creative Process," *Psychological Review* 69:220-232, May, 1962.

Ohles, John F. "Study-Hall—A Painful Anachronism," *Education Digest* 29:32-33, February, 1964.

Phillips, Gene D., ed. "Education Through Creative Expression," *Journal of Education* 143, February, 1963.

Pommer, Henry F. "For Better Minds and Smaller Classes," *Association of American Colleges* 42:532-533, December, 1956.

Ramstad, William K. "An Instructional System," *Journal of Secondary Education* 38:17-20, January, 1963.

Schilling, Harold K. "Independent Study and Research in the Undergraduate Physics Curriculum," *Journal of General Education* 14:22-37, April, 1962.

Shaw, Archibald B., et al. "Space for Individual Learning," *Overview* 4:30-40, March, 1963.

Shaw, Phillip. "Study Activities: A Checklist," *Elementary English* 36:390-394, October, 1959.

Shideler, Ernest H. "An Individualization Program," *Journal of Higher Education* 5:91-98, February, 1934.

Story, M. L. "Let's Give Winnetka Another Chance," *Educational Forum* 27: 99-102, November, 1962.

Strider, Robert E. L. "Colby January Program," *Liberal Education* 48:388-395, October, 1962.

Thacker, Margaret Spruce, and H. C. Largent. "Fairfield, Ill., High School Develops Independent Study Skills in American History," *National Association of Secondary School Principals Bulletin* 45:249-253, January, 1961.

Trump, J Lloyd. "Basic Changes Needed to Serve Individuals Better," *Educational Forum* 26:93-101, November, 1961.

——."Curriculum Changes of the Sixties," *National Association of Secondary School Principals Bulletin* 47:13-21, February, 1963.

——. "Developing a More Dynamic Junior High School Program," *ibid.* 48:129-143, March, 1964.

Vorob'ev, G. "Developing Independence and Creativity in Students," *Soviet Education* 5:41-48, September, 1963.

Washburne, Carleton. "An Eighty Year Perspective on Education," *Phi Delta Kappan* 45:145-150, December, 1963.

Watson, Goodwin. "What Psychology Can We Feel Sure About?" *Teachers' College Record* 61:253-257, February, 1960.

White, Lucien W. "Short Contributions—Independent Study of the Academic Library," *Journal of Higher Education* 33:44-47, January, 1962.

White, R. W. "Motivation Reconsidered: The Concept of Competence," *Psychological Review* 66:297-333, September, 1959.

Willcox, Isobel. "Criteria for Effective Independent Activities," *Elementary School Journal* 56:268-271, February, 1956.

Wilson, Eugene S. "The Individual Prepares for Admission to College," *National Association of Secondary School Principals Bulletin* 46:56-59, May, 1962.

Xavier, Sister Mary. "Catalysts for Scholarship," *Catholic Educational Review* 59:176-185, March, 1961.

BOOKS, DISSERTATIONS, PAMPHLETS, ETC.

Aitken, Wilford M. *The Story of the Eight-Year Study.* New York: Harper and Brothers, 1942.

Anderson, Robert H. "Organizing Groups for Instruction," *Individualizing Instruction,* Sixty-first Yearbook of the National Society for the Study of Education, Part 1. Chicago: University of Chicago Press, 1962.

Association for Supervision and Curriculum Development. *Freeing Capacity to Learn.* Washington, D.C.: National Education Association, 1960.

––––––. *New Dimensions in Learning: A Multi-Disciplinary Approach.* Washington, D.C.: National Education Associaton, 1962.

––––––. *New Insights and the Curriculum.* Washington, D.C.: National Education Association, 1963.

––––––. *Perceiving, Behaving, Becoming: A New Focus for Education.* Washington, D.C.: National Education Association, 1962.

Baskin, Samuel. "Independent Study: Methods, Programs and for Whom?" *Current Issues in Higher Education,* Proceedings of the Seventeenth Annual National Conference on Higher Education. Washington, D.C.: National Education Association, 1962.

––––––. "Quest for Quality," *New Dimensions in Higher Education* (No. 7). Washington, D.C.: U.S. Government Printing Office, 1960, OE-50016.

Beck, Robert H. "Society and Individuals," *Individualizing Instruction,* Sixty-first Yearbook of the National Society for the Study of Education, Part 1. Chicago: University of Chicago Press, 1962.

Beggs, David W., III, ed. *Team Teaching: Bold New Venture.* Bloomington: Indiana University Press, 1964.

Bonthius, Robert H., F. James Davis, and J. Garber Drushal. *The Independent Study Program in the United States.* New York: Columbia University Press, 1957.

Brickell, Henry M. *Organizing New York State for Educational Change.* Albany, N.Y.: State Education Department, University of the State of New York, 1961.

Brown, B. Frank. *The Non-Graded High School.* Englewood Cliffs, N.J.: Prentice-Hall, 1963.

Bruner, Jerome S. *On Knowing.* Cambridge, Mass.: Harvard University Press, 1962.

Bugelski, B. R. *The Psychology of Learning.* New York: Holt, Rinehart and Winston, 1956.

Cole, Luella, and Jessie Mary Ferguson. *Students' Guide to Efficient Study.* New York: Rinehart, 1946.

Conant, James B. *The Education of American Teachers.* New York: McGraw-Hill, 1963.

Craig, Robert C. *The Transfer Value of Guided Learning.* New York: Bureau of Publications, Teachers' College, Columbia University, 1953.

Deterline, William A. *An Introduction to Programmed Instruction.* Englewood Cliffs, N.J.: Prentice-Hall, 1962.

Ellsworth, Ralph E., and Hobart D. Wagener. *The School Library: Facilities for Independent Study in the Secondary School.* New York: Educational Facilities Laboratories, 1963.

Felder, Bernice Dell. "Characteristics of Independent Study Practices in Colleges and Universities of the United States." Unpublished Doctor's thesis, University of Texas, 1963.

Goodlad, John I. "Individual Differences and Vertical Organization of the School," *Individualizing Instruction,* Sixty-first Yearbook of the National Society for the Study of Education, Part 1. Chicago: University of Chicago Press, 1962.

Greeman, Gladys. *Independent Work Periods.* Washington, D.C.: Association for Childhood Education, 1961.

Griffin, William M. "A Study of the Relationship of Certain Characteristics of High School Seniors to Effectiveness in Independent Study." Unpublished Doctor's thesis, School of Education, Syracuse University, 1964.

Gruber, Howard E., et al. *Contemporary Approaches to Creative Thinking: A Symposium Held at the University of Colorado.* New York: Atherton Press, 1962.

Gruhn, William T., and Harl J. Douglass. *The Modern Junior High School.* New York: The Ronald Press, 1956.

Guilford, J. P. *Personality.* New York: McGraw-Hill, 1959.

Hatch, Winslow R., and Ann Bennett. "Independent Study," *New Dimensions in Higher Education* (Vol. 1). Washington, D.C.: U.S. Government Printing Office, 1960, OE 50005.

Hilgard, Ernest R. *Theories of Learning.* New York: Appleton-Century-Crofts, 1956.

Hutchins, Robert Maynard. *The Higher Learning in America.* New Haven, Conn.: Yale University Press, 1936.

Margarones, John Joseph. "Critical Requirements for Independent Study Based on Critical Incidents Reports by Instructors and Students." Unpublished Doctor's thesis, School of Education, Boston University, 1961.

Michaelis, John U. *Social Studies for Children in a Democracy—Recent Trends and Developments.* Englewood Cliffs, N. J.: Prentice-Hall, 1963.

National Education Association. *Schools for the Sixties*. New York: Mc-Graw-Hill, 1963.

National Society for the Study of Education. *Changes and Experiments in Liberal Arts Education*, Thirty-first Yearbook of the Society, Part 2. Bloomington, Ill.: Public School Publishing Co., 1932.

———. *Individualizing Instruction*, Sixty-first Yearbook of the Society, Part 1. Chicago: University of Chicago Press, 1962.

———. *Theories of Learning and Instruction*, Sixty-third Yearbook of the Society, Part 1. Chicago: University of Chicago Press, 1964.

New Teaching Aids for the American Classroom. Washington, D. C.: U.S. Office of Education and Institute for Communication Research, Stanford University, 1960.

Noar, Gertrude. *The Junior High School Today and Tomorrow*. Englewood Cliffs, N.J.: Prentice-Hall, 1956.

Parnes, Sidney J., and Harold F. Harding, eds. *A Source Book for Creative Thinking*. New York: Charles Scribner's Sons, 1962.

Robinson, Edgar Eugene. *Independent Study at Stanford*. Stanford, Calif.: Stanford University Press, 1937.

Shane, Harold G. "The School and Individual Differences," *Individualizing Instruction*, Sixty-first Yearbook of the National Society for the Study of Education, Part 1. Chicago: University of Chicago Press, 1962.

Shaplin, Judson T., and Henry F. Olds, eds. *Team Teaching*. New York: Harper and Row, 1964.

"Talent and Tomorrow's Teachers—The Honors Approach," *New Dimensions in Higher Education* (No. 11). Washington, D.C.: U.S. Government Printing Office, 1961.

Thelen, Herbert A. *Education and the Human Quest*. New York: Harper and Brothers, 1960.

Thorpe, L. P., and A. M. Schmuller. *Contemporary Theories of Learning*. New York: The Ronald Press, 1954.

Torrance, E. Paul, ed. *Talent and Education: Present Status and Future Directions*. Minneapolis: University of Minnesota Press, 1960.

Trump, J. Lloyd, and Dorsey Baynham. *Focus on Change: Guide to Better Schools*. Chicago: Rand McNally, 1961.

Young, Paul Thomas. *Motivation and Emotion*. New York: John Wiley and Sons, 1961.

Notes

1. J. Lloyd Trump, *Images of the Future* (Washington, D.C.: National Association of Secondary School Principals, 1959).

CHAPTER 1

1. The author once was asked by a visitor at his school, "Do you have independent study here?" It sounded more like a disease which should be discussed in the health room than a behavioral goal of education.

2. A system of relationships which accepts uniqueness in perception and thinking. Examples are found in the term paper, the original experiment, initiative, and invention. Association for Supervision and Curriculum Development, *New Insights and the Curriculum*, 1963 Yearbook (Washington, D.C.: National Education Association, 1963), p. 313.

3. An example of this is the *Chemistry Handbook: Experiments, Demonstrations and Other Activities Suggested for Chemistry* (Albany, N.Y.: State Education Department, Bureau of Secondary Curriculum Development, 1962).

4. A television comedian was heard to quip about his high school days, "I didn't learn very well; I wasn't a very good teacher."

5. J. P. Guilford, "Creativity: Its Measurement and Development," in Sydney J. Parnes and Harold F. Harding, eds., *A Source Book for Creative Thinking* (New York: Charles Scribner's Sons, 1962), pp. 157-63.

CHAPTER 2

1. Samuel Baskin, "Quest for Quality," *New Dimensions in Higher Education* (Washington, D.C.: U.S. Government Printing Office, 1960), No. 7, OE 50016, p. 3. Winslow R. Hatch and Ann Bennett, "Independent Study," is Vol. I, OE 50005.

2. Robert H. Bonthius, F. James Davis, and J. Garber Drushal, *The Independent Study Program in the United States* (New York: Columbia University Press, 1957), p. 9.

3. Edgar E. Robinson, *Independent Study at Stanford* (Stanford, Calif.: Stanford University Press, 1937).

4. *Ibid.*, p. 11.

5. W. R. Hatch and A. Bennett, "Independent Study."

6. Jacques Barzun, "Keeping Abreast of Education," *Phi Kappa Deltan*, 38 (Feb., 1937), 222.

7. R. H. Bonthius et al., *The Independent Study Program*.

8. *Ibid.*, p. 47. Table 4 is reproduced by permission.

9. J. Lloyd Trump and Dorsey Baynham, *Guide to Better Schools: Focus on Change* (Chicago: Rand McNally, 1961).

10. R. H. Bonthius et al., *The Independent Study Program*.

11. *Ibid.*

12. Willard J. Congreve, "Learning Centers . . . Catalyst for Change," *Educational Leadership*, 21, No. 4 (Jan., 1964), 211-13.

13. W. R. Hatch and A. Bennett, "Independent Study."

14. Arthur W. Chickering, "Dimensions of Independence," *Journal of Higher Education*, 35, No. 1 (Jan., 1964), 38-41.

15. *Ibid.*, 40.

16. R. H. Bonthius et al., *The Independent Study Program*, p. 67.

17. Harold G. Shane, "The School and Individual Differences," *Individualizing Instruction*, Sixty-first Yearbook, National Society for the Study of Education (Chicago: University of Chicago Press, 1962), Part 1, pp. 44-61.

18. W. R. Hatch and A. Bennett, "Independent Study," 36.

19. H. M. Brickell, *Organizing New York State*, pp. 24-47.

20. J. L. Trump and D. Baynham, *Guide to Better Schools*.

21. David W. Beggs, III, et al., *Team Teaching: Bold New Venture* (Bloomington: Indiana University Press, 1964).

22. Donald W. Huffmire, "Analysis of Independent Study Projects," *The Science Teacher*, 29, No. 3 (April, 1962), 31-39.

23. A. W. Chickering, "Dimensions of Independence."

24. Clarence Leuba, "Using Groups in Independent Study," *Improving College and University Teaching*, 12, No. 1 (Winter, 1964), 26-30.

CHAPTER 3

1. The genesis and continuation of our Freshman Project is due in large part to the vision, creativity, and perseverance of Edgar Bernstein and Ernest N. Poll, who have been with the program since its beginning.

2. Wilford M. Aitkin, *The Story of the Eight-Year Study* (New York: Harper & Brothers, 1942), p. 113.

CHAPTER 4

1. Herbert A. Thelen, *Education and the Human Quest* (New York: Harper & Brothers, 1960), p. 16.

2. For a description of the Instructional Materials Center at Lakeview

High School, see *The Decatur-Lakeview High School: A Practical Application of the Trump Plan* by David W. Beggs, III (Englewood Cliffs, N. J.: Prentice-Hall, 1964). Sketches of the building and descriptions of the program are given in detail.

Chapter 5

1. In a presentation given to the Conference on Team Teaching at the Elementary School Level, Chicago, Ill., May 7, 1964.

2. For a detailed analysis of these plans, see *Nongraded Schools: Bold New Venture*, ed. Edward G. Buffie and David W. Beggs, III, to be published by Indiana University Press.

3. J. L. Trump, *Images of the Future.*

4. The author would like to express appreciation to the following colleagues at the Indiana University Laboratory School from whom many ideas were gleaned: Mrs. Lucy Johnson, Mrs. May Kate Ambler, Mrs. Janet Groomer, Mrs. Arlene Minger, Miss Sara Smith, and Mrs. Karen Stucky.

5. Sidney P. Marland, "Winnetka's Learning Laboratory," *Educational Leadership*, 20 (April, 1963), 459-65.

6. Mildred L. Krohn, "Learning and the Learning Center," *ibid.*, 21 (Jan., 1964), 217-22.

7. Edwin A. Read and John K. Cronkovic, *The Continuous Progress Plan* (Provo, Utah: Brigham Young University, 1963).

Chapter 6

1. J. Lloyd Trump, "Developing a More Dynamic Junior High School Program," *National Association of Secondary School Principals Bulletin* (hereafter referred to as *NASSP Bulletin*), 48 (March, 1964), 131.

2. Gertrude Noar, *The Junior High School Today and Tomorrow* (Englewood Cliffs, N. J.: Prentice-Hall, 1956), p. 231.

3. J. L. Trump, "Developing a More Dynamic Junior High School Program," 134.

4. *Guide to Programmed Teaching* (General Programmed Teaching Corporation, Box 4285, Albuquerque, N. M.), p. 6.

5. E. Ross Stuckless and Jack W. Birch, "Programmed Instruction in Written Language for the Deaf," *Exceptional Children*, 30, No. 7 (March, 1964), pp. 296-303.

6. William T. Gruhn and Harl R. Douglass, *The Modern Junior High School* (2d ed.; New York: Ronald Press, 1956), pp. 31-32.

Chapter 7

1. For further information concerning the details of this type of schedule, see Chapter 6.

CHAPTER 8

1. Bruce Shertzer, *Working with Superior Students: Theories and Practices* (Chicago: Science Research Associates, 1960), pp. 131-66.

2. Perhaps independent study has a place for students with limited ability, but the content of the inquiry has bounds and requires teacher direction and more frequent consultation and supervision.

3. Jacob W. Getzels and Philip W. Jackson, *Creativity and Intelligence* (New York: John Wiley and Sons, 1961), pp. 15-28.

CHAPTER 9

1. E. B. Fry, "Programming Trends," *Audiovisual Instruction,* (April, 1961).

CHAPTER 10

1. Some significant studies have been carried out in the School Planning Laboratories at Stanford University.

2. Research along these lines is under way at Systems Development Corporation in Santa Monica, California, Stanford University, and the University of Illinois.

CHAPTER 11

1. The reading list in the Selected Bibliography of this book may be useful.

CHAPTER 12

1. Judson T. Shaplin and Henry F. Olds, Jr., eds., *Team Teaching* (New York: Harper & Row, 1964), pp. 349-51.

Index

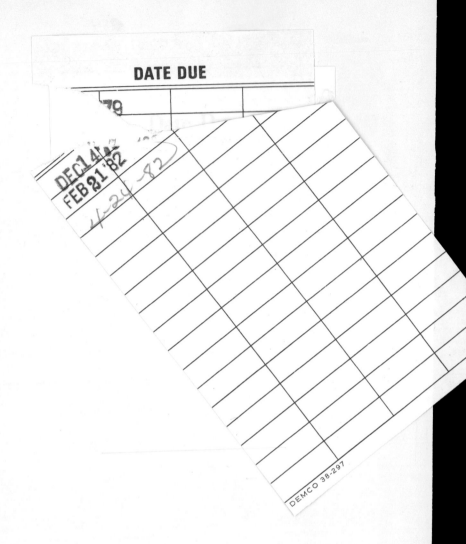